Christian Schäfer

Bringing Blockchain to Corporate Finance

A Smart Contract for Corporate Bonds

Bibliografische Information der Deutschen Nationalbibliothek:

Die Deutsche Nationalbibliothek verzeichnet diese Publikation in der Deutschen Nationalbibliografie; detaillierte bibliografische Daten sind im Internet über http://dnb.d-nb.de abrufbar.

Impressum:

Copyright © EconoBooks 2020

Ein Imprint der GRIN Publishing GmbH, München

Druck und Bindung: Books on Demand GmbH, Norderstedt, Germany

Covergestaltung: GRIN Publishing GmbH

Abstract

The objective of this master thesis is to examine the technical feasibility of a possible blockchain use case: A smart contract that enables the issuing and trading of corporate bonds without intermediaries. The key features for the smart contract have been derived from the payment mechanisms of a bond and the standard for token contracts established within the Ethereum developer community. The contract's source code is written in Solidity, an object-oriented, Turing-complete programming language, influenced by JavaScript and C, and designed for Ethereum applications. The coding and testing of the smart contract have been done in the integrated development environment Remix. The requirements for the smart contract could be implemented successfully, as confirmed by the documentation of two simulations.

Inhaltsverzeichnis

Tabellenverzeichnis

1 Introduction

A few month ago was the tenth anniversary of the Bitcoin White Paper publication. (Nakamoto (2008)) Originally intended to be an innovative electronic payment system that could redefine the meaning of the word *trust* within the financial system, it turned out that the technology Bitcoin is based on, Blockchain, could have a disruptive impact on other industries as well. (The Economist (2015)) Blockchain enthusiasts, private companies, government and academic institutions are currently trying to stake out and unlock the full spectrum of the technology's potential. (Pavlus (2018, p.58)) It is becoming apparent that the areas in which the blockchain will likely drive profound change are the financial industry, the public sector, the energy sector, the Internet of Things, the supply chain management, the medical technology or the media industry. (Schütte et al. (2017, p.6))

The financial industry is currently undertaking most of the blockchain research projects. (Schütte et al. (2017, p.27)) Capital market transactions are among the use cases that are being examined in this sector. Many players are involved in these transactions, resulting in high costs and long transaction times. By integrating blockchain technology into the settlement of security transactions, the cost and complexity of the processes might be significantly reduced and the settlement time substantially shortened as the trading parties can interact directly with each other. (Schütte et al. (2017, p.28))

The crucial instrument for the realization of these potentials are smart contracts, enabled by the Ethereum Blockchain. (Buterin (2013, p.1)) These self-executing agreements facilitate direct transactions between two parties without intermediaries and can be individually designed and set up due to Ethereum's open source nature. (Laurence (2017, p.64)) The Ethereum developer community has already programmed smart contracts for a wide variety of use cases within the financial sector and published their source codes on platforms. If you search on these platforms for smart contracts that aim to facilitate securities transactions, you will find some that cover the issuing of company shares and the management of dividend payments. (Proebsting (2018a)) However, there is a lack of smart contracts in the documentation that allow the issuance and trading of bonds. This is the starting point of this master thesis.

The requirements for the design of such a smart contract are going to be derived from the payment mechanisms of a fixed-interest corporate bond as well as from the established standard for token contracts. The smart contract will be coded and tested in the integrated development environment Remix.

The text assumes basic knowledge about blockchain technology and one of its variants, Ethereum. Therefore the thesis starts with information about smart contracts, the programming language Solidity, the concept of tokens and the established token standard ERC20 in chapter 2. The payment logic and equations for the valuation of a corporate bond are then presented in the following chapter. In Chapter 4, the requirements are derived from the previous presentations. Section 5 introduces the development environment Remix. Chapter 6 shows the contract's source code and clarifies its features. The contract is being tested by two test simulations in the seventh section. Finally, the contract is going to be discussed in chapter 8.

2 Smart Contracts

The idea of computer programs that automatically enforce agreements originated from Nick Szabo, published in 1994. (Szabo (1994)) Smart contracts, as they are called, lacked practical implementation for years, partly due to technical resource constraints. About two decades later, the founders of Ethereum took up the idea again. (Tapscott and Tapscott (2017, pp.140, 141)) In the Ethereum white paper, smart contracts are defined as programs that *"automatically move digital assets according to arbitrary pre-specified rules."* (Buterin (2013, p.1)) These value transfers not necessarily solely involve the exchange of cryptocurrency between two parties, (Antonopoulos (2017, p.275)) also realizable are interchanges of other kinds of information, like digital signatures of physical goods. Thereby Ethereum has expanded the application range of blockchain technology and increased the likelihood that it will have a deeper impact on our economy and everyday life. (Laurence (2017, pp.30, 156))

However, the most important and obvious use cases for blockchain-based smart contracts are within the finance sector. (Biryukov et al. (2017, p.2)) Successful proof-of-concept projects around the world show how securities transactions can be conducted more cost-effectively, quickly, transparently and securely in the future. (Schütte et al. (2017, pp.22, 28))

To give some examples: At the end of 2016, the German Stock Exchange and the German Bundesbank presented a blockchain prototype for the settlement of securities. (Deutsche Bundesbank and Deutsche Börse (2018, p.2)) The American stock exchange NASDAQ, enables private investors to digitally manage their securities through its blockchain application Linq. (Nasdaq (2015, p.1)) The Australian ASX Group, a major stock exchange operator, intends to settle securities via the blockchain in the near future. (wiwo.de (2017)) Last but not least, Daimler AG, in cooperation with the South German regional bank LBBW, has already documented bond placements using blockchain technology. (Atzler (2017))

Many of the proof-of-concept projects are carried out by the institutions, which theoretically could become dispensable through the blockchain. (Schütte et al. (2017, p.27)) But one of the key visions for the Ethereum project is to give as many economic actors as possible the opportunity to write the financial agreements they conclude with each other without intermediaries. (Buterin (2013, p.13)) For this reason Ethereum has an open source character and provides extensive documentation on how to write your own Smart Contracts in the programming language Solidity. (https://solidity.readthedocs.io/)

2.1 Solidity

Solidity is a high-level, Turing-complete, programming language with similarities to JavaScript and C. It is not the only language used in Ethereum applications, but currently the most common. (Dannen (2017, p.72)) Solidity is constantly evolving, but could be replaced in the future, as it has happened with predecessors. (Crypto (2019)) The most important features of Solidity used for the design of the bond contract are presented in the following paragraphs.

Functions are executable units that change the state variables of a contract. (https://solidity.readthedocs.io/ (2019a)) They are used to produce values, like numbers, or true or false statements. (Dannen (2017, p.82)) A function can be available for programs outside the contract. *Public* functions are visible externally as well as internally, one can interact with these functions via a user interface. The default visibility status of functions is *private*, meaning that the function is only visible within the current contract. (Dannen (2017, p.83)) State variables have the same possible visibilities. (https://solidity.readthedocs.io/ (2019b))

Via *Function Modifiers* the behavior of functions can be changed. As used in the bond contract, they can add a condition that must be fulfilled prior to the execution of the function. They are often used when the same lines of code are needed several times within a contract in order to write these lines only once. (https://solidity.readthedocs.io/ (2019c))

The most common value types in Solidity are Booleans, Signed and Unsigned Integers, Strings and Addresses. Booleans abbreviated with *bool* are true or false expressions. Signed integers, denoted as *int*, are negative, whereas unsigned integers, *uint*, are positive numbers. Strings are sequences of letters enclosed in double or single quotation marks. (https://solidity.readthedocs.io/ (2019d)) Each account in Ethereum is assigned to an address consisting of 20 bytes of hexadecimal characters. (Buterin (2013, p.13)) Address types have two *member types*, *transfer* and *balance*. These enable to move ether to an account or to request the balance of the account. (Dannen (2017, p.83))

Address-related keywords allow to initiate the execution of common tasks in solidity using the member types:

- *<Address>.balance* returns the balance of an address in Wei.
- *<Address>.transfer* sends a given amount of Wei to the address.
- *this.balance* outputs the balance of the current contract. (Dannen (2017, p.84))

The three complex reference types *struct, mapping* and *array* can be used to combine data of more storage than the usual 256 bits of memory. (Dannen (2017, p.84)) Structs are used to group several variables together. (https://solidity.readthedocs.io/ (2019e)) Mappings assign two values, which can be of different types, to each other. (Dannen (2017, p.84)) By specifying a key value as a parameter, a corresponding *value* is output. (https://solidity.readthedocs.io/ (2019f)) *Arrays* enable to construct lists of any type with an either fixed or dynamic number of elements. (https://solidity.readthedocs.io/ (2019g))

Global special variables are available for all Solidity smart contracts. Block or transaction properties, time or ether units are subsumed under these variables. Some examples:

- *now* displays the block's timestamp in seconds since Unix epoch
- *msg.sender* returns the address of the transaction call sender
- *msg.value* is the amount of Wei sent with the message, i.e. transaction (Dannen (2017, p.85))

The operators that have been used within the bond contract are given in the table below. (Dannen (2017, pp.86, 87))

Description	Operator
Postfix increment and decrement	++,--
Function-like call	<func>(<args...>)
Member access	<object>.<member>
Parentheses	(<statement>)
Exponentiation	**
Inequality operators	<,>,>=,<=

Description	Operator
Equality operators, does-not-equal operator	==, !=
Assignment operators	+=, -=

Table 1: Used Solidity Operators in bond contract.
Source: Dannen (2017, pp.86, 87)

2.2 Tokens

Tokens are basically a variation of a smart contract and can be considered as digital coins. (Dannen (2017, p.71)) Thus constitute a sub-currency within the applied blockchain protocol if recognized as such by the user community. They can also be utilized as *crypto assets*, representing company shares, services, physical goods or bonds, as done in the elaborated smart contract. (Dannen (2017, pp.97, 98))

The issuing of tokens within the scope of so-called ICOs (Initial Coin Offerings) is an important instrument of blockchain start-ups to generate funds. In this context, the tokens are associated with shares of the young company or vouchers for the use of its services. (European Banking Authority (2019, p.4)) Several years there were no technical standards to be met for neither these token offerings nor the token itself. (European Central Bank (2018, p.8)) In 2015 such a standard has been introduced by the smart contract developer community. (Azimdoust (2019))

2.3 ERC20 standard

With the ERC20 tokens, a uniform standard has emerged whose rules are widely accepted and adhered to by the majority of smart contract developers. (Azimdoust (2019))

The name consists of the abbreviation for "Ethereum Request for Comments" and the number of the community's attempts to create a framework for standardizing the functionalities of tokens. This set of rules aims to facilitate and unify the token development process while providing sufficient space for the development of innovative blockchain solutions and increasing usability. (https://theethereum.wiki (2018))

Azimdoust (2019) summarizes the advantages of the ERC20 standard by: *"They enable unified and quick transactions, more efficient transaction confirmations, a reduction of the contract violation risk and a more efficient and faster interaction with other tokens."*

The ERC20 standard asks for six *functions* and two *events* to be integrated in the contract. (https://theethereum.wiki (2018)) The required functions determine how tokens must be transferred and how token-related data can be accessed. *Events* contain formatting specifications for the logging of transactions in the blockchain. (www.bitdegree.org/ (2019))

The required functions:

1 A function which outputs the total amount of supplied token is required.

2 The token balance of a token owner needs to be accessible.

3 The transfer of token from one account to another has to be possible.

4 There needs to be a function that assigns a party the allowance to sell token on behalf of someone.

5 It must be possible for the entrusted party to actually assert the allowance and send the tokens on behalf of someone to a third party.

6 One should be able to have insight over how many tokens a party still has a right of disposal. (https://theethereum.wiki (2018))

The required events:

1 The token needs a logging structure that occurs when tokens have been transferred.

2 And also a logging structure, if a disposal permission was granted. (https://theethereum.wiki (2018))

The standard was adhered to during the development of the bond smart contract.

3 Corporate Bonds

In the context of this master's thesis, the word *bond* always refers to a fixed-interest corporate bond.

The logic of a bond is simple: Once the loan has been handed over to the borrower, the lender receives regular interest payments over the term of the loan. When the due date is reached, the original loan amount is repaid. (Ross et al. (2008, p.192))

A fictitious example to illustrate the payment structure and to define the key figures of a bond: Company X considers to borrow 400,000 € for 5 years, spread on 10 bonds. In order to attract borrower, X needs to pay interest on the loan and competes with other investment opportunities. Company X decides to give 5 percent interest per year, since this is the assumed corresponding interest rate offered by similar companies for similar debt issued. Thus, Company X pays 0.05 * 400,000 € = 20,000 € interest per annum during the 5-year term of the bonds. At the end of the fifth period X will repay the 400,000 € to the lender, 40,000 € per bond. (Ross et al. (2008, p.193)) The annual payment of 2,000 € interests per bond from X to the investors is the bond's *coupon*. The *coupon rate* is equal to the coupon paid every year divided by the face value. Based on the example the equation delivers 2,000 € / 40,000 € = 0.05 or 5 percent as coupon rate. The amount that an investor loans to X per bond and gets repaid at the end is called *face value*, *par value* or *nominal value* of a bond. The maturity represents the date on which the nominal value is repaid to the lender. (Ross et al. (2008, p.193)) The cash flow for each bond is:

	Period 1	Period 2	Period 3	Period 4	Period 5
Coupon	2,000 €	2,000 €	2,000 €	2,000 €	2,000 €
Face value					40,000 €
Total	2,000 €	2,000 €	2,000 €	2,000 €	42,000 €

Table 2: Cumulative coupon payments from issuer to investor after each period.

What happens when the market interest rate changes within the term and the owner considers to trade the bond? Since the cash flow of a bond stays the same over the whole term, a changing market interest rate results in a fluctuating value of the bond. Assuming a raising interest rate, the present value of the bond's cash flow decreases, thus the bond's worth shrinks. Vice versa, a lower interest rate leads to an appreciation of the bond. The influential factors for the current value of a bond's cash flow are the remaining time until maturity, the face value, the coupon, and the interest rate given for bonds with alike key data. (Ross et al. (2008, p.193))

Our example:

There are 4 years left to maturity and the market interest rate raises to 6 percent. How does this affect the present value of the bond?

Present value = € 40,000 / 1.06⁴ = € 40,000 / 1.2625 = 31,683.75 €

The bond cash flow is worth:

Annuity present value = € 2,000 * (1 – 1/1.06⁴) / 0.06 = 6,930.21 €

Added together one receives the bond's present value of:

Total bond value = 31,683.75 €+ 6,930.21 € = 38,613.96 €

The reason why the bond now sells for less than the 40,000 € face value is that the coupon rate of the bond lies one percentage point below the market interest rate. It would be rational for investors to purchase Company X's bonds, when they are compensated for the annual coupon loss. A balancing effect is reached by a lower price. (Ross et al. (2008, pp.194, 195))

Combining the separate equations for determining the present value of the bond, one generates a general expression for a bond's value:

$$Bond\ value = C * \frac{\left[1 - \frac{1}{(1+r)^t}\right]}{r} + \frac{F}{(1+r)^t} \qquad [3.1]$$

C is the coupon paid per period, r refers to the market interest rate, t is equal to the periods remaining to maturity and F is the face value of the bond.

The first summand equals the calculation for the present value of the bonds, the second corresponds to the present value of the face value. (Ross et al. (2008, p.196))

In addition to the price of a bond, the yield, or the effective rate, plays a key role in the purchase decision of the potential buyer. Calculated by the equation below:

$$e = \frac{c}{p} + \frac{100 - p}{p * t} \qquad [3.2]$$

The coupon rate in percent is denoted with c, p is equal to the purchase price of the bond in percent of the face value and t, again, refers to the remaining periods to maturity. (Altrogge (1996, p.127))

3.1 and 3.2 have been used in the developed bond contract.

4 Requirements for the Smart Contract

The contract should meet the following list of requirements resulting from the transaction mechanisms of a corporate bond, while complying with the ERC20 standard in order to gain community acceptance and achieve high usability. Note, that these are mere technical requirements for the smart contract's source code. Legal aspects to be considered for the authorization to offer a technical product for financial services have not been taken into account for the preparation of this thesis.

1. The issuer is able to input the issuing volume, the face value, the coupon interest rate, and the term as bond key data.

2. Two types of bond transactions are enabled, firstly between the issuer and an investor and secondly between two investors. The purchaser receives a digital representation of a bond, a token, in return for providing the seller with the corresponding bond value in Ether.

3. The contract allows the issuer to make recurring coupon interests payments.

4. The contract allows the issuer to transfer the face values back to the investors at maturity.

5 Remix

The Remix compiler is a browser- based Integrated Development Environment (IDE) for smart contracts. (https://theethereum.wiki (2017)) Remix facilitates developer to write, deploy and interact with smart contracts, and has been used to develop and test the bond contract. (https://remix.readthedocs.io/en/latest/ (2019a)) The following paragraphs shall introduce the most important features of Remix.

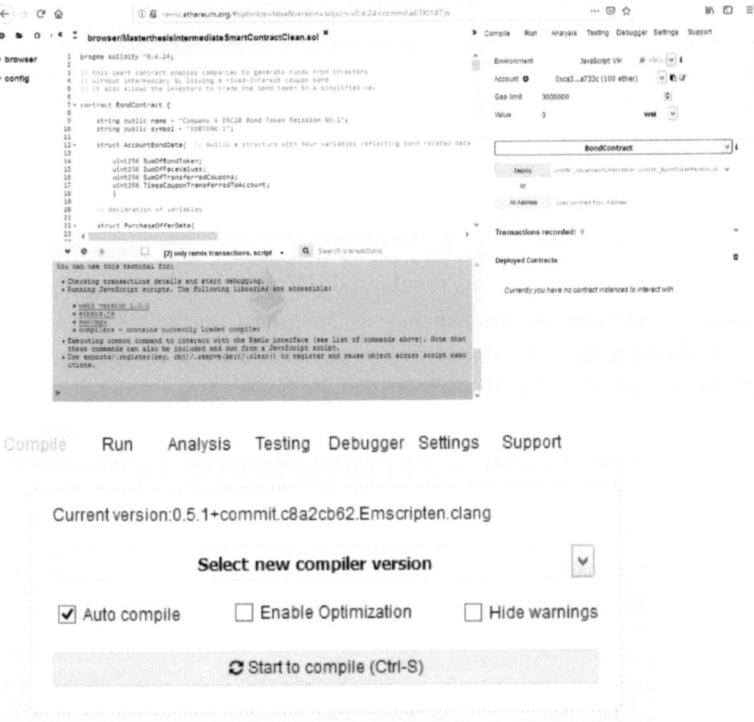

In order to create a new contract the developer opens a new Solidity file, by clicking on the plus symbol in the upper left corner. (https://remix.readthedocs.io/en/latest/ (2019d)) The developer needs to select a Solidity version by clicking on the "Compile" tab and choosing the desired version in the list. The chosen version in the compiler tab has to be identical to the version given in your first code line. (https://remix.readthedocs.io/en/latest/ (2019c)) By choosing "Auto compile", each time when the smart contract code is changed, remix recompiles anew. Syntax errors or warnings are shown in the editor next to the code line numbering. (https://remix.readthedocs.io/en/latest/ (2019b))

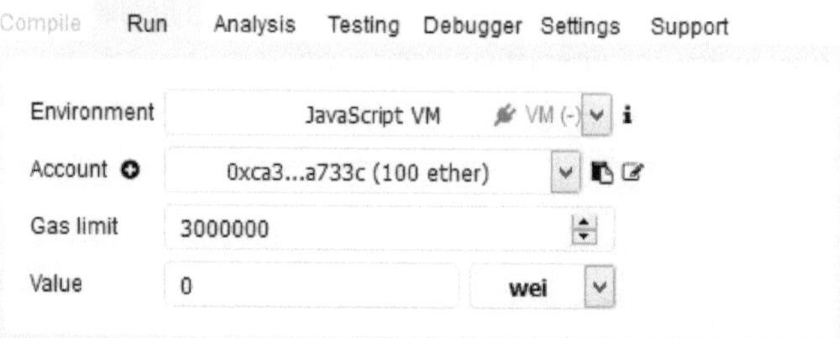

In the *Run* tab one can choose between three environments, *Injected Web3*, *Web3 provider* and *JavaScript VM*. The first two environments require that Remix is plugged to one of the following external tools: An *Ethereum Node, Mist* or *Meta-mask.* (https://remix.readthedocs.io/en/latest/ (2019e)) For the development of the bond contract the *JavaScript VM* has been selected. In this environment all transaction will be passed to a sandbox blockchain in the browser, which is recreated every time when you reload the page, no transaction will be persistent. Below *Environment*, in the *Account* field, five test addresses are selectable, initialized with 100 Ether each. If needed, more test accounts can be added. The *Gas limit* for each transaction in Remix defaults to 3,000,000. Underneath the *Gas limit* section, one can set the Ether *Value* attached to a transaction. After every transaction this value is reset to 0. There are also smaller Ether units that can be picked. The unit *Wei* for instance, which is the smallest unit of the currency Ether. One Ether is equal to a Quintillion Wei (10^{18}). Solidity calculates and displays all currency transactions in *Wei* by default. (https://remix.readthedocs.io/en/latest/ (2019f))

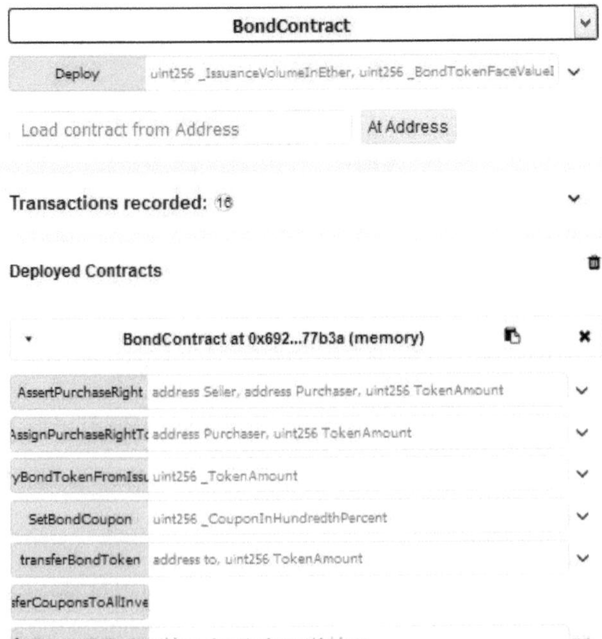

Below the *Value* field is the section where new instances can be created. Via *Deploy* the developer can send a transaction into the sandbox blockchain that creates a new instance of the contract type which is selected in the contract list. When the constructor function of the contract needs parameters as arguments, the developer has to specify them in the line next to the *Deploy* button. In the section *Deployed Contracts* the developer can interact with the implemented contract and try out whether the integrated function work in the desired way. Red buttons represent functions that modify the state of the blockchain. Blue buttons only retrieve the data of the contract, clicking them does not create a new transaction and thus does not change the state of the blockchain. (https://remix.readthedocs.io/en/latest/ (2019f))

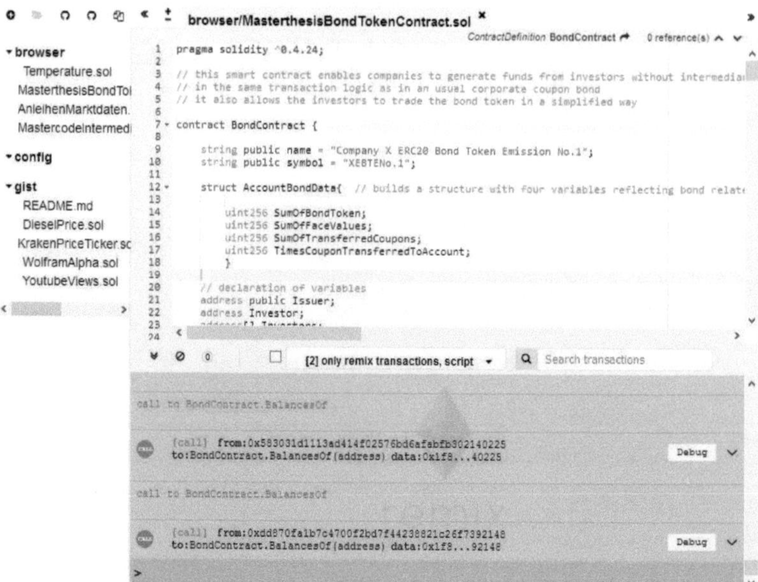

The terminal, below the code editor, displays a message whether the transaction has been mined successfully and could be added to the sandbox blockchain. Validating the transaction can take several seconds, in which the terminal signalizes that it is in a pending state.

The file explorer on the left lists all Solidity files stored in the developer's browser. It also contains contract files that have been imported by one of the contracts, for instance parent contracts for the usage of oracle services. The developer can rename, delete or add a new file in this section. (https://remix.readthedocs.io/en/latest/ (2019d))

6 The Bond Token Smart Contract

This section introduces the program code of the developed smart contract and explains its functions. The complete program code can be found in the appendix.

The screenshots in this chapter were taken in the open source text editor *Atom* for better readability and not in the *Remix* IDE, where the actual coding took place.

```
1    pragma solidity ^0.4.24;
2
3    // this smart contract enables companies to generate funds from investors
4    // without intermediary by issuing a blockchain equivalent to a fixed-interest
5    // corporate bond, it also allows the investors to trade the bond token
6
7    contract BondContract {
```

The syntax of the first line specifies that the source code is written for Solidity version 0.4.24. As already stated in the Remix chapter, this version has to be consistent with the selected compiler version in the "Settings" section. The seventh line commands the creation of a contract with the name *BondContract*, which in the following is also called *Bond Token Smart Contract* or *Bond Token Contract*. (https://solidity.readthedocs.io/ (2019h))

```
12   struct AccountBondData{   // builds a structure with four variables
13       // reflecting bond related data of each investor account
14       uint256 SumOfBondToken;
15       uint256 SumOfFaceValues;
16       uint256 SumOfTransferredCoupons;
17       uint256 TimesCouponTransferredToAccount;
18   }
19   mapping(address=>AccountBondData) public BalancesOf;
```

The combination of the *struct AccountBondData* and the *mapping BalancesOf* store bond data and link it to an investor's account. It connects four variables, of type unsigned integer with 256 bytes, grouped together by the *struct*, to one Ethereum address. The mapping has a visibility status *public*, in order to make the values of the *struct* variables accessible and to meet the second required function of the EC20 standard. The first variable of the *struct*, *SumOfBondToken*, records the number of all bonds held by a single account. The second variable, *SumOfFaceValues*, represents the total of all bond's face values assigned to an account. The third variable contains the amount of coupon interests, which has been transferred to an investor's address, memorized by the *SumOfTransferredCoupons* variable. The fourth variable within the *struct*, *TimesCouponTransferredToAccount*, serves as counter variable for how often the coupon payments have already been made. (Will it Scale-Channel (2017a))

```solidity
struct PurchaseOfferData{
    uint256 AmountOfOfferedBondToken;
    uint256 TradingPricePerBondTokenInWei;
    uint256 Yield;
}
mapping(address => mapping(address => PurchaseOfferData)) public MyOfferData;
```

A second *struct*, *PurchaseOfferData*, serves as storage for trade relevant data. This *struct* contains the amount of offered token, denoted as *AmountOfOfferedBondToken*, the trading price per *Bond Token*, represented by the variable *TradingPricePerBondTokenInWei*, and the *Yield* that could be realized by taking the offer. Data within the *struct* is changed with the help of the mapping *MyOfferData*, which connects the *struct* data with two addresses, the potential seller's and purchaser's address. (Will it Scale-Channel (2017a))

The lines subsequent to the second *struct* and before the constructor function are used for the declaration of variables. (https://solidity.readthedocs.io/ (2019i)) In order to keep the length of the thesis within reasonable limits and due to their triviality, the declaration is not documented and explained here, and can instead be studied in the appendix.

```solidity
constructor(uint256 _IssuanceVolumeInEther, uint256 _BondTokenFaceValueInEther,
    uint256 _CouponInPercent, uint256 _TermInYears) public payable {
```

The contract is being built and deployed in the sandbox blockchain via the *constructor* function. The issuing company inputs four arguments: The issuance volume, and the nominal value, both given in *Ether*, the coupon rate in percent and the term of the bond, given in years. The visibility is set to public, obviously, since the function needs to be accessible for it's users. (https://solidity.readthedocs.io/ (2019j)) The constructor is also *payable*, making it possible for the function to receive Ether. The state changing expressions of a function are enclosed in curly brackets. (https://solidity.readthedocs.io/ (2019k))

```solidity
Issuer = msg.sender;
LeftToReachIssuanceVolumeGoalInWei = safeMultiplication(_IssuanceVolumeInEther,(uint256(10) ** decimals));
IssuanceVolumeInWei = safeMultiplication(_IssuanceVolumeInEther,(uint256(10) ** decimals));
BondTokenFaceValueInWei = safeMultiplication(_BondTokenFaceValueInEther,(uint256(10) ** decimals));
BondTokenFaceValueInEther = _BondTokenFaceValueInEther;
BondTokenCouponInPercent = _CouponInPercent;
```

The lines within the curly brackets of the constructor function process the inputs passed by the initiator. The input parameters are being transformed from a temporary variable into a permanent state variable and converted from Ether to Wei, the unit in which Solidity does currency related calculations. Each expression is terminated by a semicolon. *Msg.sender* refers to the address that initiated a function call. (Dannen (2017, p.85)) The initiator of the constructor function is assigned to the variable *Issuer. SafeMultiplication* and *SafeAddition* are used to prevent calculations from an integer overflow. (Dourlens (2017)) The arguments within the brackets are the products, of the multiplication, respectively the summands of the addition. The *decimals* variable is set to 18 to convert the currency bearing variables from Ether to Wei, such that the term *(uint256(10) ** decimals)* is equal to ten to the power of eighteen, the conversion rate from Ether to Wei. Two parameters are getting converted into Wei. The *IssuanceVolumeInEther* and the *BondTokenFaceValueInEther* variable. (Proebsting (2018a))

```
70   TermInYears = _TermInYears;
71   TermInSeconds = safeMultiplication(TermInYears, 365 days);
72   MaturityDateInSecondsSinceUnixEpoch = safeAddition(now, TermInSeconds);
73   EndOfTokensSale = safeAddition(TimeOfContractCreation,1 days);
74   TotalBondTokenSupply = safeDivision(IssuanceVolumeInWei, BondTokenFaceValueInWei);
75   BalancesOf[Issuer].SumOfBondToken = TotalBondTokenSupply;
```

Still within the *constructor* function, the maturity of the Bond Tokens is calculated in the Solidity supported time format *seconds since the UNIX epoch,* i.e. Solidity does all time related computing in seconds. (solidity.readthedocs.io/ (2019l)) The UNIX time started at 00:00:00 UTC on January 1st 1970. (solidity.readthedocs.io/ (2019k)) Also, the end of the Bond Token sale is determined. The code within the constructor function also creates new tokens, each representing one bond, denoted as *Bond Token*. The amount of disposable Bond Tokens is calculated by the division (*safeDivision*) of the issuance volume and the Bond Token face value, and gets stored in the *public* variable *TotalBondTokenSupply,* leading to the fulfillment of the first required function for the ERC20 standard. Initially the code assigns all tokens to the issuer's account address. (Proebsting (2018b)) The syntax for updating a specific struct variable is shown in the last line of the screenshot above. It is composed of the mapping name, followed by the key value of the mapping put in square brackets, and a dot followed by the name of the variable. This sequence is equaled to the new value. (Will it Scale-Channel (2017a))

```
73   function BuyBondTokenFromIssuer(uint256 _TokenAmount) public
74       payable returns(bool success) {
```

The function *BuyBondTokenFromIssuer* is one of the key features within the contract. With this function the contract fulfils the third of the required functions for the ERC20 standard. It takes one argument of type uint256, the amount of Bond Tokens the purchaser aims to acquire. This function obviously demands to be *payable*, allowing the Bond-Token-owner-to-be to attach the required Ether amount as transaction price. When all conditions within the function are met, the terminal outputs "True" as signal that the transaction has been successful. (https://solidity.readthedocs.io/ (2019k))

```
77    TransactionPrice = safeMultiplication(BondTokenFaceValueInWei, _TokenAmount);
78
79    require(LeftToReachIssuanceVolumeGoalInWei>=TransactionPrice);
80    require(TransactionPrice == msg.value);
81    require(now <= EndOfTokensSale);
```

Within the *BuyBondTokenFromIssuer* function code lines the transaction price is calculated as product of the face value and the token amount. Furthermore there are three conditions that must be fulfilled for processing the function, reflected by the three *require* statements. 1. The transaction price needs to be equal or less than the remaining amount of Ether that the issuer aims to collect. 2. The Ether value that is attached to the function call needs to equal the transaction price. 3. The token sale has not ended yet. (Proebsting (2018b))

```
85    var investor = BalancesOf[msg.sender];
86    investor.SumOfFaceValues += TransactionPrice;
87    investor.SumOfBondToken += _TokenAmount;
88    BalancesOf[Issuer].SumOfBondToken -= _TokenAmount;

95    Investors.push(msg.sender);
```

The lines of the above screenshot update the data of the struct variables *SumOfFaceValues* and *SumOfBondToken* of the issuer's as well as of the investor's account. The temporary variable *investor* acts as a shortcut for the sequence of the mapping *BalancesOf* and the *msg.sender* as *key value*. *Investors.push(msg.sender)* adds the address of the message sender as new entry in the *Investors* array. (Will it Scale-Channel (2017a))

```
119    function TransferCouponsToAllInvestors () public OnlyIssuer returns(bool success){
120        n = Investors.length;
121        for(uint256 i=0;i<n;i++){
122        Investor = Investors[i];
123        require(BalancesOf[Investor].TimesCouponTransferredToAccount<TermInYears);
124        TransferAmount = safeDivision((safeMultiplication(
125            BalancesOf[Investor].SumOfFaceValues,(BondTokenCouponInPercent))),100);
126        Investor.transfer(TransferAmount);
127        BalancesOf[Investor].SumOfTransferredCoupons += TransferAmount;
128        BalancesOf[Investor].TimesCouponTransferredToAccount += 1;}
129        return true;}
```

TransferCouponsToAllInvestors enables the issuer to transfer the coupon interests to all investors at once. In addition to this function it is also possible to transfer the coupons to only one investor, presented at the end of this chapter. Both functions can only be called by the issuer, which is ensured by the function modifier *OnlyIssuer*, also shown in more detail at the end of the chapter. (Will it Scale-Channel (2017b)) A for-loop runs through all elements of the array investors, and allows to transfers the calculated coupon amount to the Ether account and edit the balances of each lender. (Will it Scale-Channel (2017c)) This smart contract is designed for one coupon payment per year, i.e. the number of coupon transfers must not exceed the term in years, which is guaranteed by the *require* expression. The transfer amount is equal to the product of the account's sum of face values and the coupon rate in percent divided by 100. *Investor.transfer(TransferAmount)* is the command for the actual remittance. The adjustments of the struct balances *SumOfTransferredCoupons* and *TimesCouponTransferredToAccount* of each of the financiers are done by the third and second last lines of the above screenshot.

```
139    function TransferFaceValuesToAllInvestors () public OnlyIssuer returns(bool success){
140        require(now>= MaturityDateInSecondsSinceUnixEpoch);
141        n = Investors.length;
142        for(uint256 i=0;i<n;i++){
143        Investor = Investors[i];
144        TransferAmount = BalancesOf[Investor].SumOfFaceValues;
145        Investor.transfer(TransferAmount);
146        BalancesOf[Investor].SumOfFaceValues -= TransferAmount;
147        BalancesOf[Issuer].SumOfBondToken += BalancesOf[Investor].SumOfBondToken;
148        BalancesOf[Investor].SumOfBondToken = 0;}
149        return true;}
```

As for the transfer-of-coupons-feature before, the contract shall allow the issuer to transfer the face values back to all investors at once at maturity. The *require* function aims to prevent from executing the function before maturity. A for-loop is used to make sure that each account address, that is element in the list of investors, receives back the loan. The *TransferAmount* variable, this time, is equal to the face values associated with the account. The last lines of the function, again, update the balances of the *AccountBondData* struct. The *SumOfFaceValues* is reduced by the transferred amount. And all Bond Token the investor has held before the maturity date are assigned to the issuer again.

```
162     mapping(address => mapping(address => uint256)) public PurchaseRight;

164   function AssignPurchaseRightTo(address Purchaser, uint256 TokenAmount,
165       uint256 TradingPricePerBondTokenInEther) public returns (bool success) {
166     require(TokenAmount <= BalancesOf[msg.sender].SumOfBondToken);
167     PurchaseRight[msg.sender][Purchaser] = TokenAmount;
168     BondTokenTradingPriceInWei = safeMultiplication(TradingPricePerBondTokenInEther,(uint256(10) ** decimals));
169     BondTokenTradingPriceInPercent = safeDivision(safeMultiplication(BondTokenTradingPriceInWei, 100),
170     BondTokenFaceValueInWei);
171     RemainingTermInYears = (MaturityDateInSecondsSinceUnixEpoch - now) / 365 days;
```

The following lines of code implement a trading feature into the contract, established by two functions. The first step for trading a Bond Token between two parties is the allocation of a "purchase right" to a potential buyer by a token owner. The *AssignPurchaseRightTo* function provides this option. The fulfillment of the fourth function of the ERC20 standard is also provided by this function. The caller of the function, hence the potential seller, has to pass three arguments. The address of the potential purchaser, the amount of token he is willing to sell, as well as the price for one Bond Token in Ether. If the seller is rational, he will take formula 3.1 from chapter 3 to calculate the price of the Bond Token. A require function assures that the potential seller, the message sender, actually owns the amount of Bond Token he is willing to hand over. The *PurchaseRight* mapping documents that there exists a token allocation from a potential seller to a potential purchaser. Since the visibility of the *PurchaseRight* mapping is public, it is accessible for the contract user, therefore the sixth required function for the ERC20 standard is met. The last three equations calculate intermediate results necessary for computing the offer data. (Will it Scale-Channel (2017d))

```
173     MyOfferData[msg.sender][Purchaser].AmountOfOfferedBondToken = TokenAmount;
174     if (BondTokenTradingPriceInWei == 0){
175       MyOfferData[msg.sender][Purchaser].TradingPriceInWei = BondTokenFaceValueInWei;}
176     else {MyOfferData[msg.sender][Purchaser].TradingPriceInWei = BondTokenTradingPriceInWei;}
177     MyOfferData[msg.sender][Purchaser].Yield = (((BondTokenCouponInPercent) + (
178       (100 - BondTokenTradingPriceInPercent)/ RemainingTermInYears)) * 100) / BondTokenTradingPriceInPercent;
```

The equations above specify the results for the *PuchaseOfferData* struct variables *AmountOfOfferedBondToken*, *TradingPriceInWei* and *Yield* and assign the values to the variables. The if-condition checks whether a trading price was given, if this is not the case, the face value of the bond is taken as price. The yield is calculated by formula 3.2 given in chapter 3. (Will it Scale-Channel (2017d))

```
165    function AssertPurchaseRight(address Seller, address Purchaser, uint256 TokenAmount)
166        public payable returns (bool success) {
167
168    require(Seller != Purchaser);
169    require(Purchaser != address(0));
170    require(TokenAmount <= PurchaseRight[Seller][Purchaser]);
171    if (BondTokenTradingPriceInWei == 0){
172        require(msg.value >= safeMultiplication(TokenAmount, BondTokenFaceValueInWei));}
173    else require(msg.value >= safeMultiplication(TokenAmount, BondTokenTradingPriceInWei));
```

The second step of trading a Bond Token: With the call of *AssertPurchaseRight* the buyer, or a representative of him, actually pulls the option to buy all, or at least some, tokens offered to him. By this function, the third and the fifth of the ERC20 standard functions are provided, what means that all required functions are implemented in the contract. The purchase option is realized by giving three inputs, the addresses of the seller, and the purchaser and the amount of token he would like to acquire. The *require* conditions ensure that the purchaser and the seller are not identical, that the purchaser owns a hexadecimal address and that it is not possible to purchase more token than the purchase right includes. The if-condition checks whether the seller assigned a value for the variable *BondTokenTradingPriceInWei* and guarantees that the purchaser sends enough Ether in the case that the variable is unequal to zero and for the case that the face value is taken as price for the bond.

```
175    BalancesOf[Seller].SumOfBondToken -= TokenAmount;
176    BalancesOf[Seller].SumOfFaceValues -= safeMultiplication(TokenAmount, BondTokenFaceValueInWei);
177    BalancesOf[Purchaser].SumOfBondToken += TokenAmount;
178    BalancesOf[Purchaser].SumOfFaceValues += safeMultiplication(TokenAmount, BondTokenFaceValueInWei);
179    PurchaseRight[Seller][Purchaser] -= TokenAmount;
180    Seller.transfer(msg.value);
```

The lines on the above screenshot, still within the *AssertPurchaseRight* function, adjust the account balances within the *AccountBondData* struct for the seller and the purchaser after the trade. Two struct variables are affected by the trade for both parties, the *SumOfBondToken* and the *SumOfFaceValues*. The second last line updates the *PurchaseRight* mapping. The last line of this function actually transfers the price for the traded tokens to the seller. (Dannen (2017, p.86, 87))

```solidity
    function transferBondToken(address to, uint256 TokenAmount) public returns(bool success) {
        require(BalancesOf[msg.sender].SumOfBondToken >= TokenAmount);
        BalancesOf[msg.sender].SumOfBondToken -= TokenAmount;
        BalancesOf[to].SumOfBondToken += TokenAmount;


        BalancesOf[msg.sender].SumOfFaceValues -= TokenAmount*BondTokenFaceValueInWei;
        BalancesOf[to].SumOfFaceValues += TokenAmount*BondTokenFaceValueInWei;
```

Also in order to meet the standards for an ERC20 token, the function *transferBondToken* allows to send Bond Token to an investor without receiving Ether in return, i.e. it allows to donate token. (Will it Scale-Channel (2017d)) It takes two arguments, the beneficiary's address and the number of token. The *require* condition guarantees that the initiator of the transaction, the message sender, possesses enough tokens. The subsequent lines modify the *AccoundBondData* variables *SumOfBondToken* and *SumOfFaceValues* of the donor and the receiver of the donation.

```solidity
    // gives the contract's Ether balance
    function ContractEtherBalance() public view returns (uint256) {
        return address(this).balance;
    }


    // enables the issuer withdraw Ether from the contract
    function WithdrawalOfContractOwner(uint256 WithdrawAmountInWei) public
      OnlyIssuer returns(bool success){
        msg.sender.transfer(WithdrawAmountInWei);


        return true;
    }
```

Each smart contract has an own Ether balance. The *ContractEtherBalance* function enable to check this balance. In order to actually pull the collected funds out of the contract the *WithdrawalOfContractOwner* function allows the issuer to withdraw Ether out of the contract and transfer the amount to his own account. The function takes the amount of Ether as argument. (Dannen (2017, p.88))

```solidity
    function CountInvestors() view public returns (uint) {
        return Investors.length;
    }

    function ListOfInvestors() public view returns(address[]) {
        return Investors;
    }
```

These functions return the number of investors and the list of all investors.

```
229    // enables issuer to transfer Ether to contract
230    function TransferEtherToContract () public payable OnlyIssuer {
231    }
```

TransferEtherToContract allows the issuer to provide the contract with funds again before he transfers the coupons and face values to the investors.

```
257  function safeMultiplication(uint256 a, uint256 b) internal pure returns (uint256) {
258      if (a == 0) {
259          return 0;
260      } else {
261          uint256 c = a * b;
262          assert(c / a == b);
263          return c;}}
```

```
266  function safeDivision(uint256 a, uint256 b) internal pure returns (uint256) {
267      // Solidity only automatically asserts when dividing by 0
268      require(b > 0);
269      uint256 c = a / b;
270      assert(a == b * c + a % b); // There is no case in which this doesn't hold
271      return c;}
```

```
274  function safeAddition(uint256 a, uint256 b) internal pure returns (uint256) {
275      uint256 c = a + b;
276      require(c >= a);
277      return c;}
```

SafeMultiplication, *SafeDivision* and *SafeAddition* prevent the calculations from integer overflow. Integer overflows occur when a calculation reaches the maximum or minimum size of a type. The 256 bits of the type uint256 for instance, can hold values from 0 to 2^256. (Dourlens (2017))

```
262    // integration in other functions ensures that only the issuer can call this function
263    modifier OnlyIssuer() {
264        require(msg.sender == Issuer);
265        _;
266    }
```

OnlyIssuer is a modifier function. In solidity a modifier is a piece of code which can be called by other functions. They are useful when the same lines of code need to be executed several times within a contract. In the case of the bond contract the condition that the message sender is the issuer of the contract occurs multiple times and could be written only once thanks to the modifier. (Will it Scale-Channel (2017b))

```
106   function TransferCouponsToOneInvestor(address _InvestorAccountAddress)
107     public OnlyIssuer returns(bool success){
108         var investor = BalancesOf[_InvestorAccountAddress];
109         Investor = _InvestorAccountAddress;
110         require(BalancesOf[Investor].TimesCouponTransferredToAccount<TermInYears);
111         TransferAmount = safeDivision((safeMultiplication(
112           BalancesOf[Investor].SumOfFaceValues,(BondTokenCouponInPercent))),100);
113         Investor.transfer(TransferAmount);
114         investor.SumOfTransferredCoupons += TransferAmount;
115         investor.TimesCouponTransferredToAccount += 1;
116         return true;}
```

To provide the contract with more flexibility, it also allows to transfer the coupons
for one period to only one specific account. Instead of a for-loop to pick each listed
investor and adjust the variables of the struct, only one investor is affected. The
function *TransferCouponsToOneInvestor* takes the benefiting investor as argument.

```
126   function TransferFaceValueToOneInvestor (address _InvestorAccountAddress)
127         public OnlyIssuer returns(bool success){
128         require(now>= MaturityDateInSecondsSinceUnixEpoch);
129         var investor = BalancesOf[_InvestorAccountAddress];
130         Investor = _InvestorAccountAddress;
131         TransferAmount = investor.SumOfFaceValues;
132         Investor.transfer(TransferAmount);
133         investor.SumOfFaceValues -= TransferAmount;
134         BalancesOf[Issuer].SumOfBondToken += investor.SumOfBondToken;
135         investor.SumOfBondToken = 0;
136         return true;}
```

Analog to the coupon transfer feature the issuer can also transfer the face value to
a single investor. It transfers the whole amount of Bond Token face values assigned
to the investor and adjusts the struct balances of the face value variable as well as
the token variable.

```
56   event BondPurchaseFromIssuer(address Investor, uint256 TokenAmount, uint256 BondsTotalValue);
57   event AssignedRight(address Owner, address Beneficiary, uint256 TokenAmount);
58   event BondTransferBetweenInvestors(address Seller, address Buyer, uint256 TokenAmount);
```

In order to meet the ERC20 standard the necessary events are implemented in the
functions *BuyBondTokenFromIssuer*, *AssignPurchaseRightTo*, *AssertPurchaseRight*
and *transferBondToken*. The events are defined in the beginning of the contracts
source code by the above syntaxes. (Proebsting (2018b))

```
100    emit BondPurchaseFromIssuer(msg.sender, _TokenAmount,TransactionPrice);
```

```
183    emit AssignedRight(msg.sender, Purchaser, TokenAmount);
```

```
213    emit BondTransferBetweenInvestors(Seller, Purchaser, TokenAmount);
```

```
229    emit BondTransferBetweenInvestors(msg.sender, to, TokenAmount);
```

The call of the events within the four functions is integrated by the syntax in the four screenshots above. (Proebsting (2018b))

In order to test the functionalities, two simulations are performed and documented in the next chapter.

7 Simulations

In order to verify the programed functionalities of the contract, two simulations are run using Remix. The first simulation serves as analysis of the functionalities for the issuance feature of the contract. Using simulation two, the second key feature, the trade functionality, is put to test. The screenshots in this chapter were all taken in the Remix IDE. (remix.ethereum.org/) The values used in both simulations are purely fictional.

7.1 Simulation one

- *Company X* aims to finance 400 Ether by issuing fixed-rate corporate bonds.
- The nominal value of a bond amounts to 5 Ether.
- The coupon interest rate is 5 percent.
- The term is 5 years.
- Four investors, *A*, *B*, *C* and *D*, purchase bonds.
- *A* buys 2 bonds for 10 Ether. *B* buys 4 bonds for 20 Ether. *C* buys 6 token for 30 Ether and *D* buys 8 token for 40 Ether.
- Once a fictive year passed, the coupons are paid by the issuer.
- All investors hold their purchased bonds until maturity date, resulting in the sequence of payments from the issuer to the investors given in table 3 and the cumulative coupon payments in table 4.
- The face values are paid back after the fictive fifth period.

Time Investor	After pe- riod 1	After pe- riod 2	After pe- riod 3	After pe- riod 4	After pe- riod 5
A	0.5	0.5	0.5	0.5	10.5
B	1	1	1	1	21
C	1.5	1.5	1.5	1.5	31.5
D	2	2	2	2	42

Table 3: Cash flow in Ether per investor and period.

Time Investor	After period 1	After period 2	After period 3	After period 4	After period 5
A	0.5	1	1.5	2	2.5
B	1	2	3	4	5
C	1.5	3	4.5	6	7.5
D	2	4	6	8	10

Table 4: Cumulative coupon payments in Ether per investor and period.

In the following the screenshots of the simulation in Remix are presented.

The source code displayed in the previous chapter is inserted in the code editor in Remix. Via the *Compile* tab the compiler version is chosen according to the Solidity version given in the first line of the code.

The Ethereum wallet address 0xca35b7d915458ef540ade6068dfe2f44e8fa733c acts as the issuer, company X.

The remaining four addresses given in the Remix IDE serve as investor accounts. The hexadecimal *0x14723a09acff6d2a60dcdf7aa4aff308fddc160c* will be denoted in the following as *investor A, 0x4b0897b0513fdc7c541b6d9d7e929c4e5364d2db* belongs to *investor B, 0x583031d1113ad414f02576bd6afabfb302140225* is owned by *investor C* and *0xdd870fa1b7c4700f2bd7f44238821c26f7392148* is hold by *investor D*.

The issuer deploys the contract by entering the four necessary parameters and a click on "Deploy". 1. 400 Ether issue volume. 2. The face value of one Bond Token, 5 Ether. 3. The coupon rate of 5 percent. 4. The term of the bond, 5 years.

A new Bond Contract with the hexadecimal address *0x692a70d2e424a56d2c6c27aa97d1a86395877b3a* is now implemented in the sandbox blockchain, and appears within the *Deployed Contracts* section.

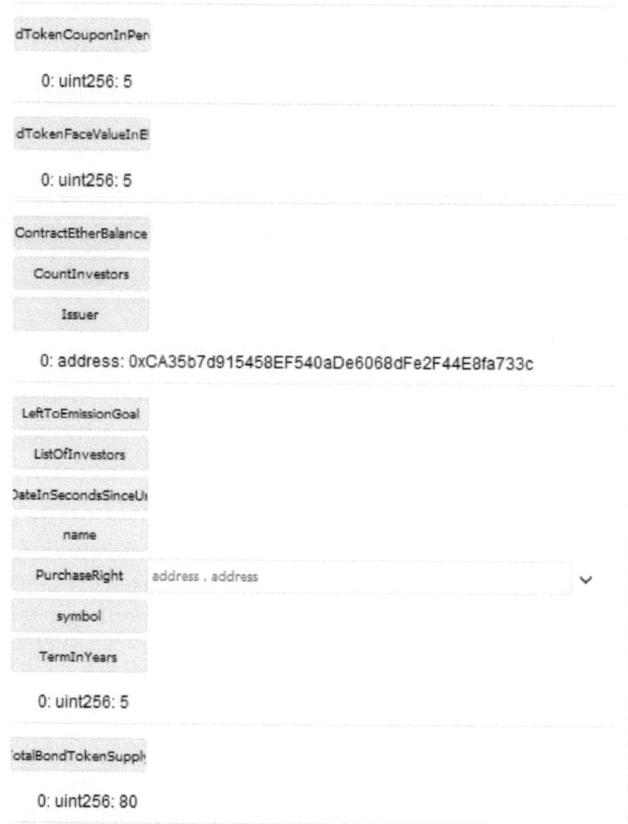

After the contract is deployed, the issuer address checks whether the bond's key data has been implemented successfully into the blockchain. In order to do so, the issuer pushes the blue *TotalBondTokenSupply* button. (https://solidity.readthedocs.io/ (2019b)) This function was implemented in order to provide the first required function for the ERC20 standard. The calculated amount equals 80 token, what is generated by the division of 400 by 5, the numbers for the issuance volume and the Bond Token face value. The *Issuer* button outputs the address of the contract creator. The account wallet address of *company X*, "0xca35b7d915458ef540ade6068dfe2f44e8fa733c", is shown. Furthermore the issuer checks whether the bonds face value, the coupon interests and the term have been implemented correctly by pushing the *BondTokenFaceValueInEther*, *BondTokenCouponInPercent* and *TermInYears* fields. Each display "5". As documented by the screenshot above the values were passed and computed correctly by the contract.

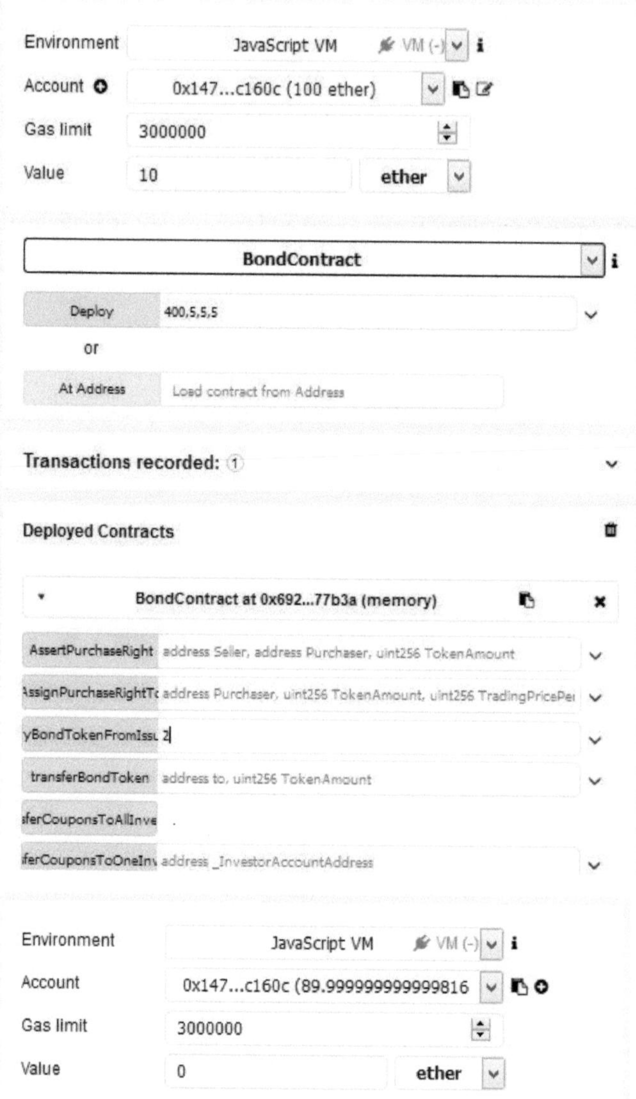

Now *investor A* buys two Bond Token by attaching 10 Ether as transaction value to the message, and passing the parameter 2 next to the *BuyBondTokenFromIssuer* button. *Investor A* started, as all test accounts, with an account balance of 100 Ether. After subtracting 20 Ether for the tokens and about 140,466 Wei of transaction costs, 89,999 Ether remain in *investor A*'s account after the purchase.

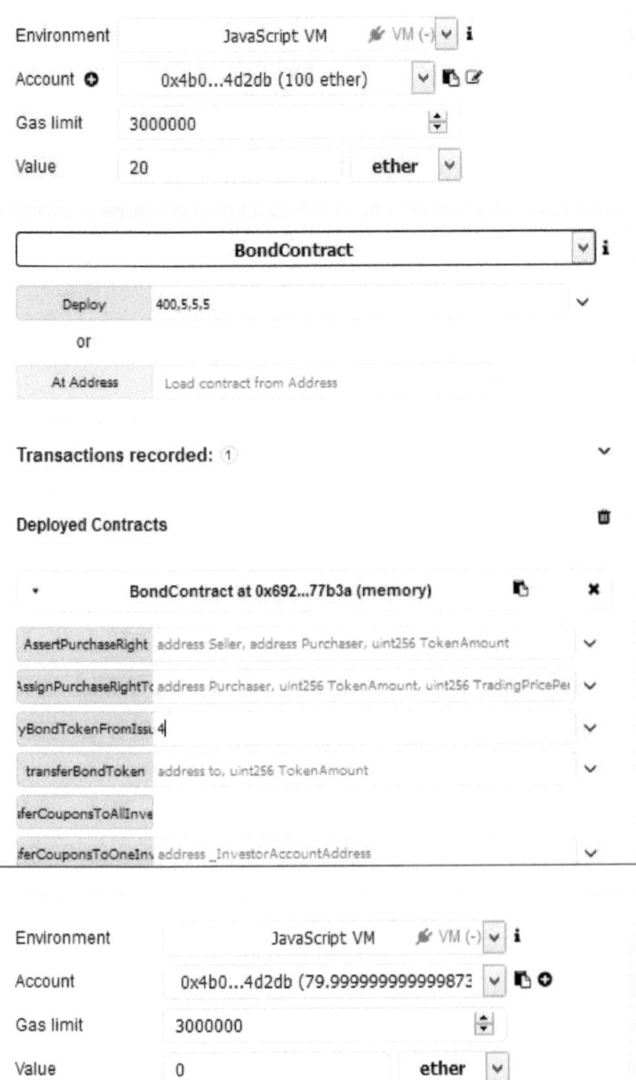

Following the same procedure *B* invests 20 Ether and receives corresponding 4 Bond Token in return, resulting in an Ether account balance of 79.999 Ether.

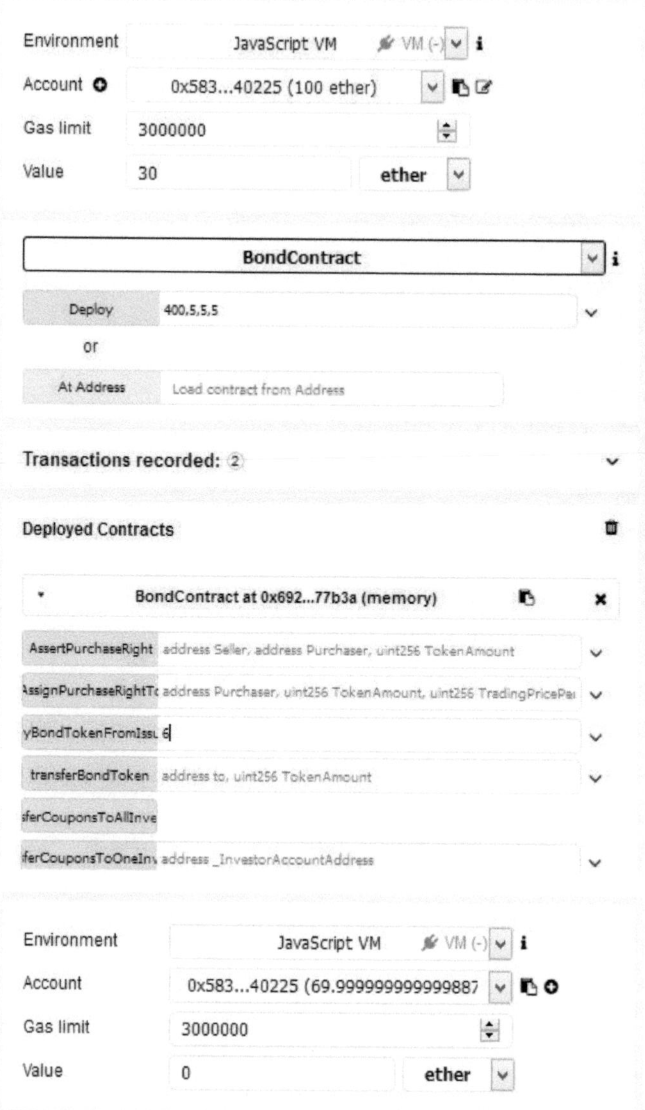

Investor C purchases 6 Bond Token for 30 Ether and has 69.999 Ether left in his account after the transaction.

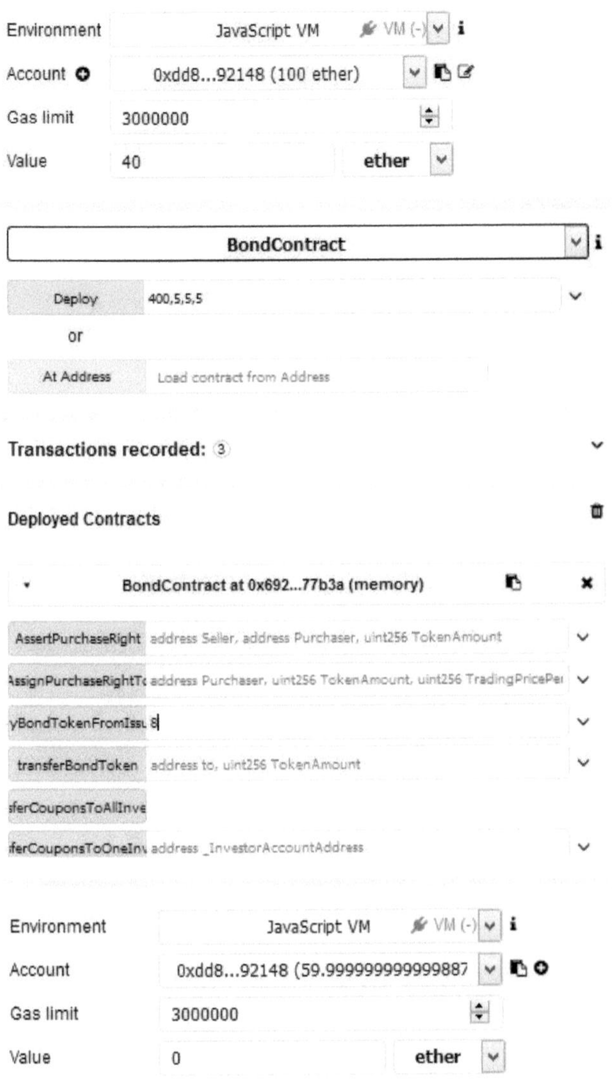

And *investor D* acquires 8 Bond Token, paying 40 Ether for them. His Ether account balance include 59.999 Ether.

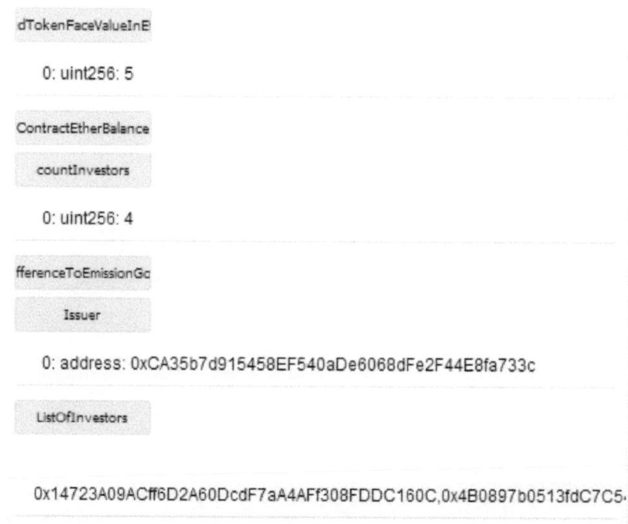

By pushing the *countInvestors* button the issuer checks whether the contract source code calculated the correct amount of four investors. By clicking *ListOfInvestors* the issuer checks whether the array of investors has been constructed successfully. Several functions rely on the array. The button section on the right does not render the list properly, therefore a screenshot of the terminal message has been taken to prove that the list is compiled correctly. (https://remix.readthedocs.io/en/latest/ (2019g))

To verify whether all tokens have been properly credited and the accounts balances have been assigned correctly to the accounts, one passes the addresses one by one and pushes the *BalancesOf* button. The *BalancesOf* function was implemented in order to provide the second required function for the ERC20 standard. With a correct value for the variable *SumOfBondToken* it is implicitly shown, that also the third required function for the ERC20 standard is integrated.

The balances of *A* display *2* as *SumOfBondToken* and 10,000,000,000,000,000,000 Wei (= 10 Ether) as *SumOfBondFaceValue.* The second variable is given in Wei out of uniformity reasons, since the value below, *SumOfCouponTransferredToAccount,* is also given in Ether. All calculations of values within the contracts are processed in Wei. It is the smallest unit of Ether, 1 Ether correspond to 10^{18} Wei. (https://theethereum.wiki (2017))

Investor B possesses *4* Bond Tokens and 20,000,000,000,000,000,000 Wei (= 20 Ether) as total face values.

Furthermore the contract accounts *6* Bond Token and 30,000,000,000,000,000,000 Wei (= 30 Ether) as *SumOfBondFaceValue* for *C.*

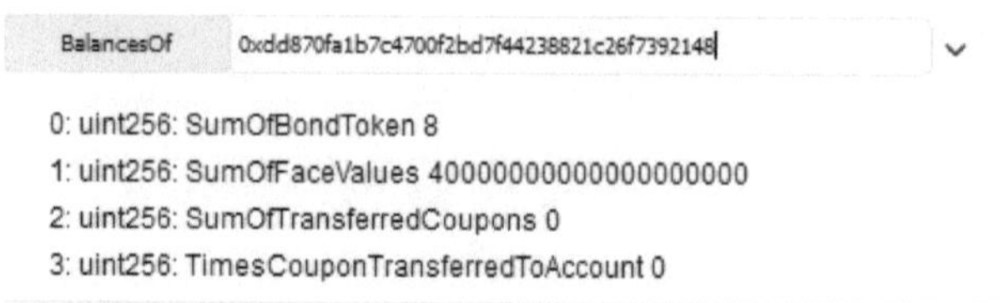

D owns 8 Bond Token and 40,000,000,000,000,000,000 Wei (= 40 Ether) in face values after the purchase.

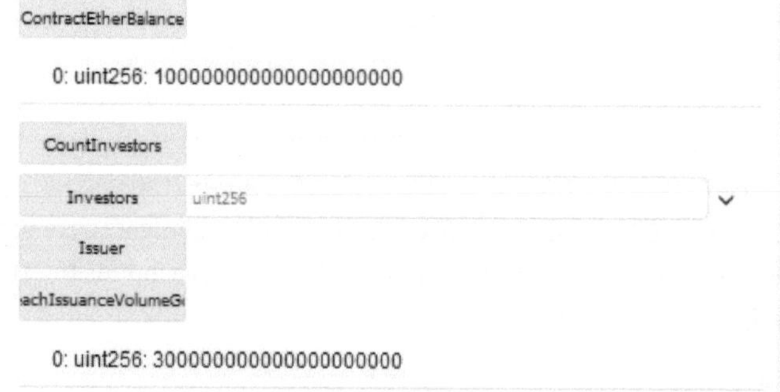

The *issuer* can also verify the contract's Ether balance with the *ContractEtherBalance* button. The amount equals 100,000,000,000,000,000,000 Wei (= 100 Ether). The contract's source code also allows to check how much there is still left to meet the issuance volume goal. Calling the *LeftToReachIssuanceVolumeGoal* function displays an amount of 300,000,000,000,000,000,000 Wei (= 300 Ether).

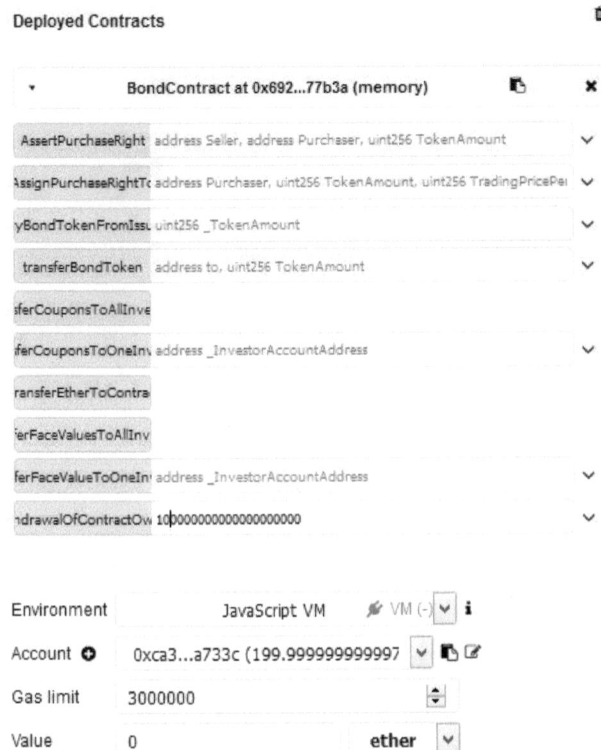

In order to transfer the collected funds from the contracts account to his own, the issuer uses the function *WithdrawalOfContractOwner*. The amount of how much Ether he would like to remove is passed as parameter. After the transfer of the whole amount, his balance sums up to 199.999 Ether.

Assuming the first year passed, the issuer transfers the coupon interests of the first period to the investors. In order to provide the contract creator with a high degree of flexibility, there are two options to ensure that within the bond contract: Option one credits the year's coupons to all investors at once. Option two allows the issuer to make a payment to a specific investor. Option one is verified in this simulation.

Before the issuer can transfer the coupon rates to the investors, he needs to supply the contract with Ether. Therefore he sends 30 Ether back to the contract's address by attaching the value to the transaction initiated by the *TransferEtherToContract* function.

Afterwards the issuer clicks on the button *TransferCouponsToAllInvestors* to allocate the coupons.

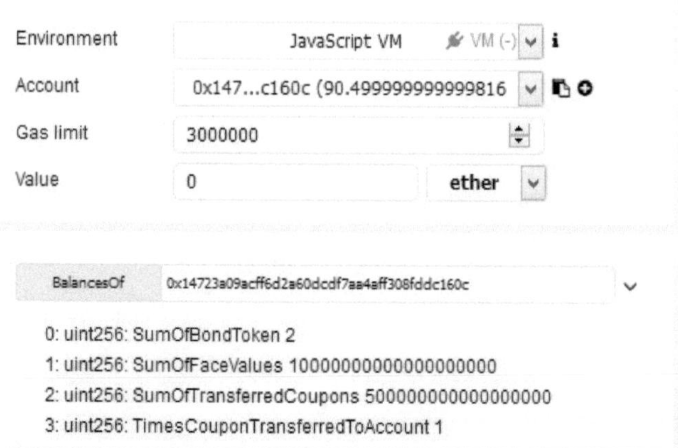

For *investor A*, the *SumOfBondToken* and the *SumOfFaceValues* obviously remain on the same level as before the coupon allocation. The *SumOfTransferredCoupons* amounts 500,000,000,000,000,000 Wei (= 0.5 Ether) and is thus identical to the value indicated by tables 2 and 3. *Investor A's* Ether account balance increases by the same amount up to 90.499 ($\approx$100-10+0.5). The *TimesCouponTransferredToAccount* variable equals one. It serves as auxiliary variable for the issuer.

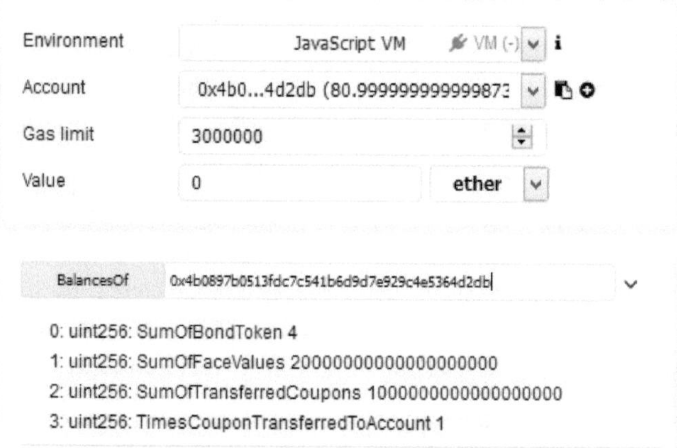

For *investor B*, the two variables that should have changed its state, equal 1,000,000,000,000,000,000 Wei (= 1 Ether) in the case of

SumOfTransferredCoupons and *1* in the case of the variable *TimesCouponTransferredToAccount*. His Ether account balance went up by 1 Ether to 80.999 Ether (≈100-20+1). This happens according to the derived results of table 3 and 4 in the beginning of the chapter.

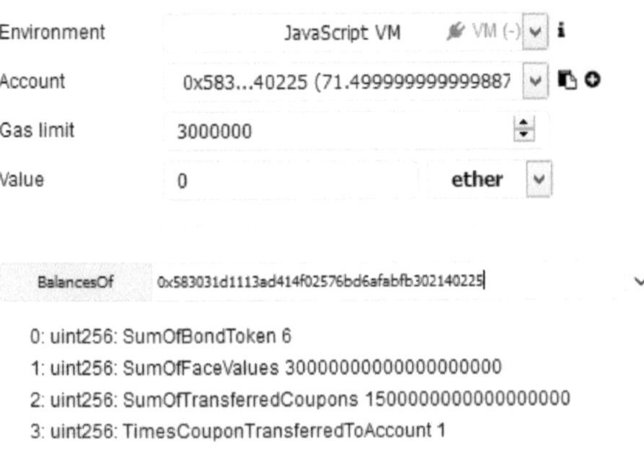

For *investor C* the altered variables are equal to 1,500,000,000,000,000,000 Wei (= 1.5 Ether) for the *SumOfTransferredCoupon* and *1* for *TimesCouponTransferredToAccount*. *C*'s account balance shows an amount of 71.499 Ether (≈100-30+1.5).

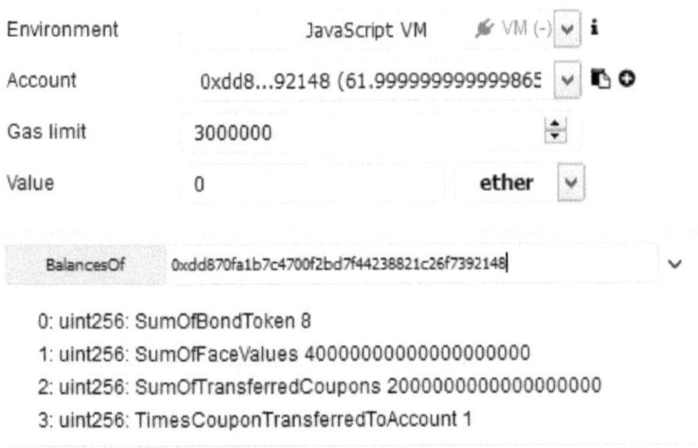

And for *investor D* 2,000,000,000,000,000,000 Wei (= 2 Ether) are credited to him as *SumOfTransferredCoupon* and *1* for *TimesCouponTransferredToAccount*. *D*'s account balance shows an amount of 61.999 Ether (≈100-40+2)

The process of documenting the coupons payments and the checking of the account balances of the investors for each period is not repeated here. The correctness of the *Bond Contract's* calculations will implicitly be verified by the results after transferring the amounts at maturity.

Assumed that the date of maturity has arrived, without the repayment of the face value, but including all coupon payments, the balances of the investors display the following values.

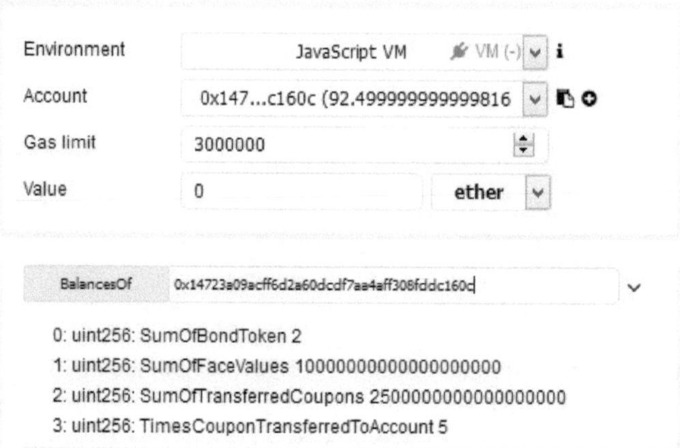

For *investor A* the altered balances are: The account balance equals 92.499 Ether. The counter variable *TimesCouponTransferredToAccount* displays 5, suggesting that coupon payments has been undertaken after each period. The total of *SumOfTransferredCoupons* amounts to 2.5 Ether, which is the exact amount, which the calculations in table 4 indicate.

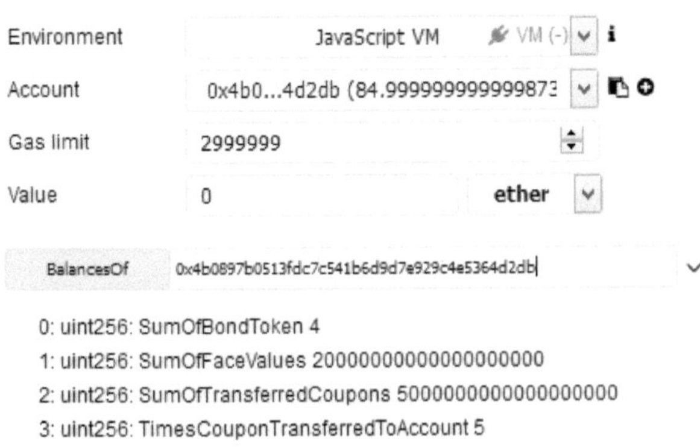

Investor B's altered balances cover an account balance of 84.999 Ether. The counter variable *TimesCouponTransferredToAccount* displays *5*. The total for the *SumOfTransferredCoupon* amounts to 5 Ether, equivalent to $5*10^{18}$ Wei, which is the exact amount, indicated by table 4, where the cumulative coupon payments are summed up.

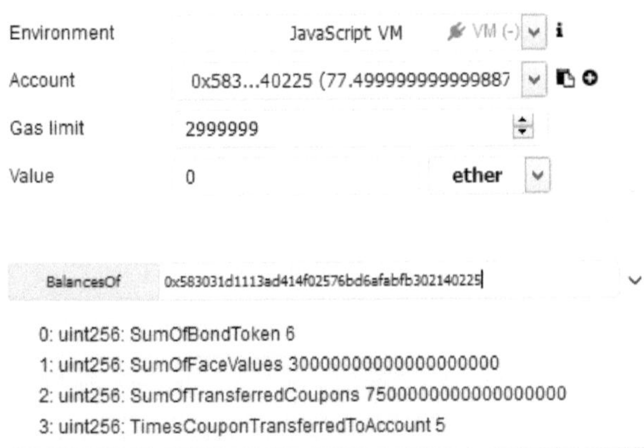

Investor C's altered balances include 77.499 Ether in his account balance. The counter variable *TimesCouponTransferredToAccount* displays *5*. The total for *SumOfTransferredCoupon* amounts to 7.5 Ether, also indicated by table 4.

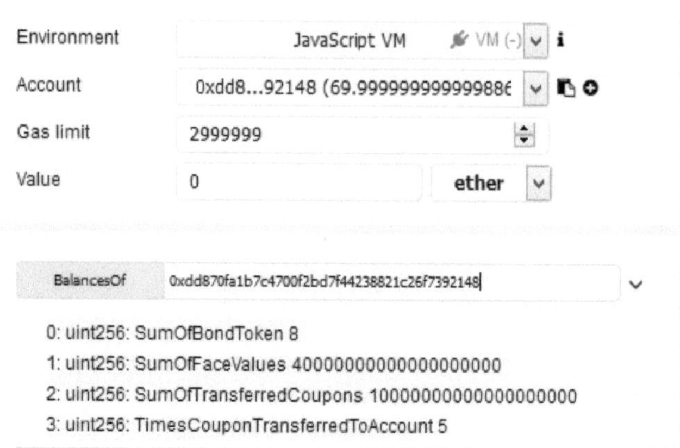

Investor D's Ether account balance equals 69.999. The counter variable *TimesCouponTransferredToAccount* display *5*. And the total for the *SumOfTransferredCoupons* amounts 10 Ether (= $10*10^{18}$ Wei), also indicated by table 4, where the coupon payments are added together.

After transferring the face values, by executing the *TransferFaceValuesToAllInvestors* function, the balances display:

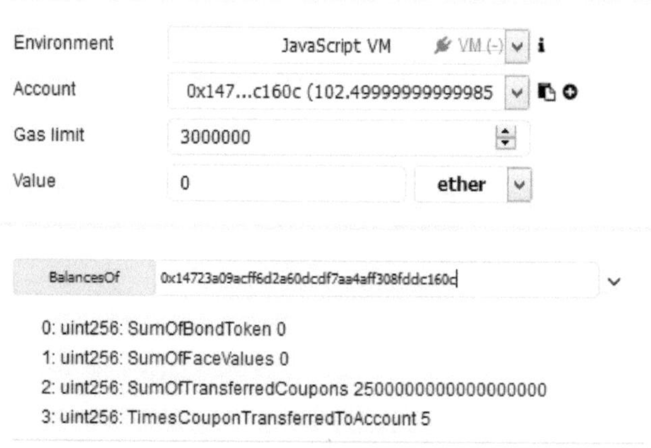

Investor A's account balance displays 102.499 Ether and *SumOfTransferredCoupons* is 2.5 Ether. Since *A* started with 100 Ether before the investment, it means, that *A's* cumulated coupon payments equal 2.5 Ether, as indicated by table 4. The other variables that should have changed within the last function call *SumOfBondToken* and the *SumOfFaceValue* equal zero, because *A* does not own a Bond Token of *Company X* anymore.

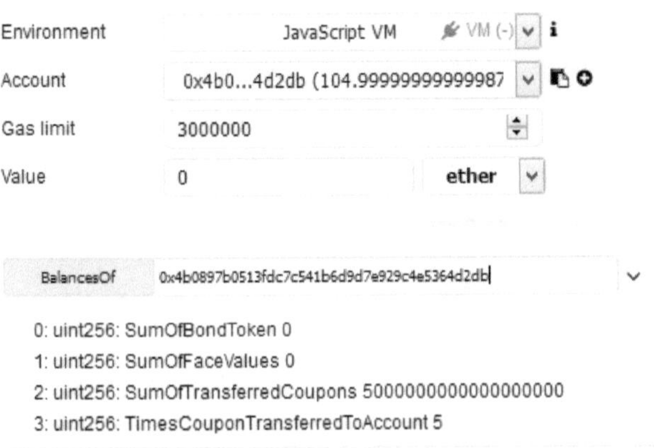

For *investor B* the final balances display 104.999 Ether as account deposits and *5* Ether as total of credited coupons. The variables *SumOfBondToken* and the *SumOfFaceValue* equal zero.

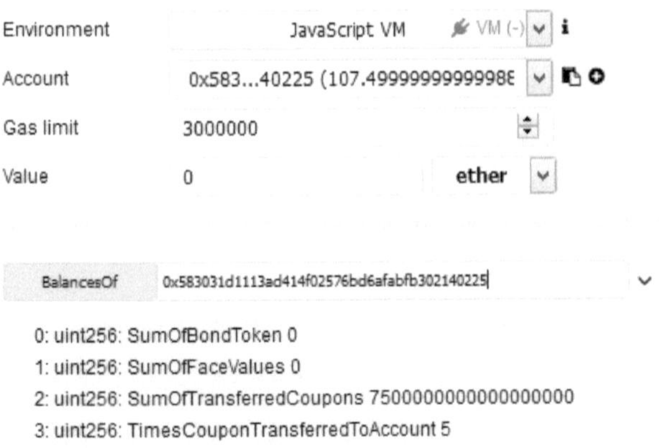

For *investor C* the final balances display 107.499 Ether as saved ether funds. Resulting in an increase of *C*'s total net wealth of about 7.5 Ether, also calculated by table 4. The *SumOfBondToken* and the *SumOfFaceValue* equal zero, as they are supposed to, since during the last transaction *C* has given up ownership of his 6 Bond Token.

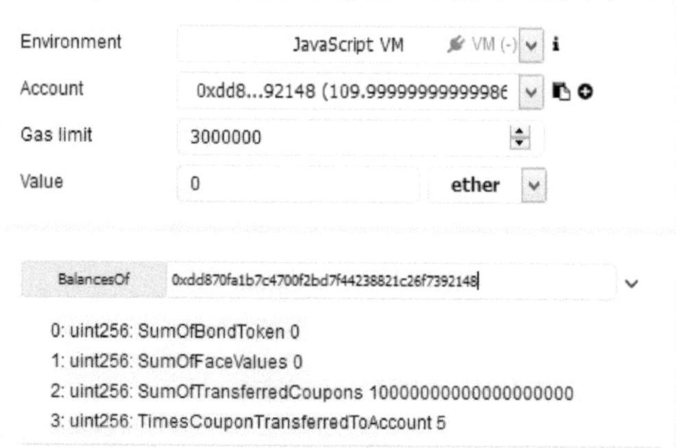

Investor D's account balance shows 109.999 Ether. The cumulated coupons payments amounted about 10 Ether, also given in table 4. The variables that should have changed *SumOfBondToken* and the *SumOfFaceValue* equal zero, as they should.

The result of the first simulation is that the issuance feature of the bond is implemented successfully into the contract.

7.2 Simulation two

This simulation tests whether the Bond Contract meet the requirements of the trade functionality and while complying with the ERC20 standard. The Bond Token key data is the same as in the first simulation:

- *Company X* aims to finance 400 Ether by issuing fixed-rate corporate bonds.

- The nominal value of one bond amounts to 5 Ether.

- The coupon interest rate is 5 percent.

- The term is set to 5 years.

- Four investors, *A, B, C* and *D*, purchase the bonds.

- A buys 2 bonds for 10 Ether. B buys 4 bonds for 20 Ether. C buys 6 token for 30 Ether and D buys 8 token for 40 Ether.

- The face values are paid back after the simulated fifth period.

- Coupons are paid once per simulated year.

- This time, after 2.5 years, A and B trade token. A buys one token from B, paying him 4 Ether for the token, plus 0.125 Ether, corresponding to the coupon revenues of a half year. Since *A* and *B* exchange the Bond Token in the midst of a period, A needs to compensate B for the loss of coupon interests for the one token, A is going to receive from the issuer instead of B after the third period. The loss amounts to the half of a coupon payment for one token in one year. Therefore A compensates B by paying 0.125 Ether more than the price of the token.

Time Investor	After period 1	After period 2	After period 3	After period 4	After period 5
A	0.5	0.5	0.75	0.75	15.75
B	1	1	0.75	0.75	15.75
C	1.5	1.5	1.5	1.5	31.5
D	2	2	2	2	42

Table 5: Cash flow in Ether per investor and period.

Time Investor	After period 1	After period 2	After period 3	After period 4	After period 5
A	0.5	1	1.75	2.5	3.25
B	1	2	2.75	3.5	4.25
C	1.5	3	4.5	6	7.5
D	2	4	6	8	10

Table 6: Cumulative coupon payments in Ether per investor and period.

The steps of the contract creation by *company X*, the purchase of the tokens by the investors A, B, C and D, as well as the crediting of the coupons for the first two periods, are the same as for simulation one and thus are not documented again at this point.

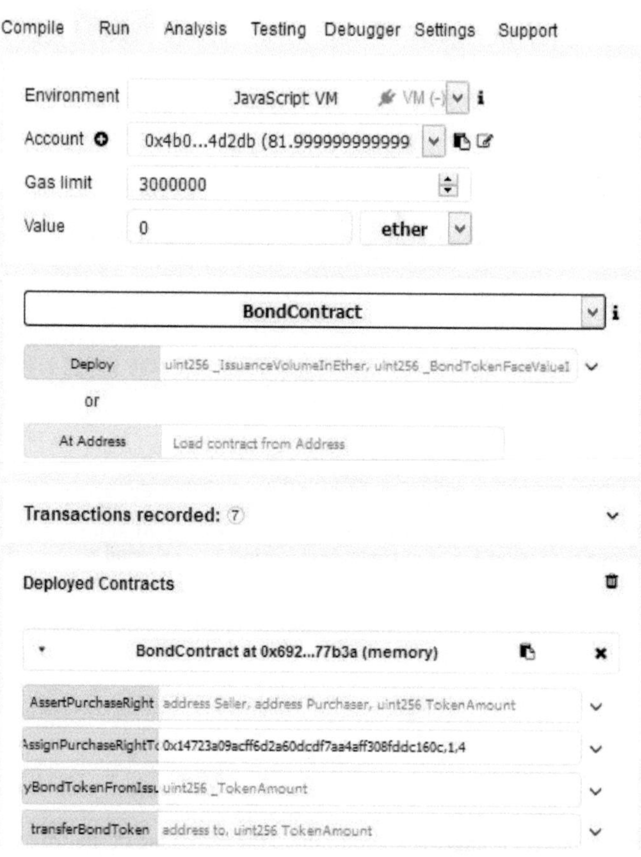

Compile   Run   Analysis   Testing   Debugger   Settings   Support
Environment   JavaScript VM   VM (-)   i
Account   0x4b0...4d2db (81.999999999999   i
Gas limit   3000000
Value   0   ether
BondContract   i
Deploy   uint256 _IssuanceVolumeInEther, uint256 _BondTokenFaceValueI
or
At Address   Load contract from Address
Transactions recorded: 7
Deployed Contracts
BondContract at 0x692...77b3a (memory)
AssertPurchaseRight   address Seller, address Purchaser, uint256 TokenAmount
AssignPurchaseRightT   0x14723a09acff6d2a60dcdf7aa4aff308fddc160c,1,4
yBondTokenFromIssu   uint256 _TokenAmount
transferBondToken   address to, uint256 TokenAmount
logs
[
  {
    "from": "0x5c3c1540dfcd795b0aca58a496e3c30fe2405b07",
    "topic": "0xa5585020673ed8882fa16ea0d173e0b551a33e1399
9519ece99ca5339570f94a",
    "event": "AssignedRight",
    "args": {
      "0": "0x4B0897b0513fdC7C541B6d9D7E929C4e5364D2
dB",
      "1": "0x14723A09ACff6D2A60DcdF7aA4AFf308FDDC16
0C",
      "2": "1",
      "Owner": "0x4B0897b0513fdC7C541B6d9D7E929C4e53
64D2dB",
      "Beneficiary": "0x14723A09ACff6D2A60DcdF7aA4AF
f308FDDC160C",
      "TokenAmount": "1",
      "length": 3
    }
  }
]

Assuming that 2.5 years after the contract creation have passed, in order to trade token via this contract, the potential seller needs to grant a purchase right to the potential purchaser about the amount of token he is willing to sell. The Bond Contract provides this by the function *AssignPurchaseRightTo*. It asks for three input parameters. The first input is the purchasers account address, *investor A*'s hexadecimal. The second is the amount of token the seller is willing to hand over, equal to 1 Bond Token in this simulation. The third is the price in Ether, *B* would like to obtain, for one Bond, 4 Ether. The function must be called by the seller, *investor B*. By a successful processing of *AssignPurchaseRightTo* the fourth required function and event 2 of the ERC20 is met.

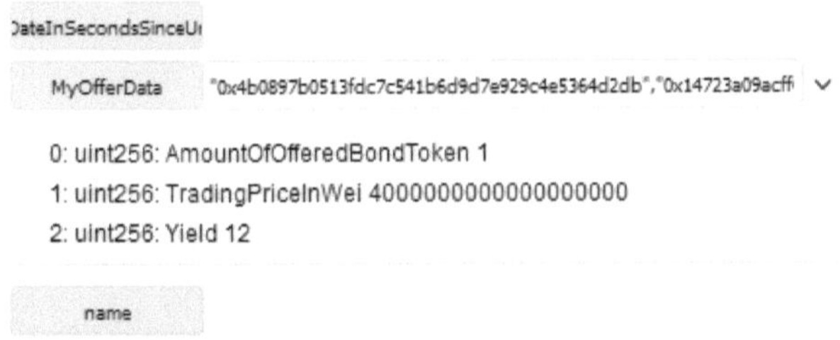

The Bond Contract enables the user to check the data of trading options, required by the sixth ERC20 standard function. The getter of *MyOfferData* returns the amount of purchasable Bond Tokens, the bond price in Wei and the corresponding yield by giving the seller's and the purchaser's addresses as inputs in this very sequence.

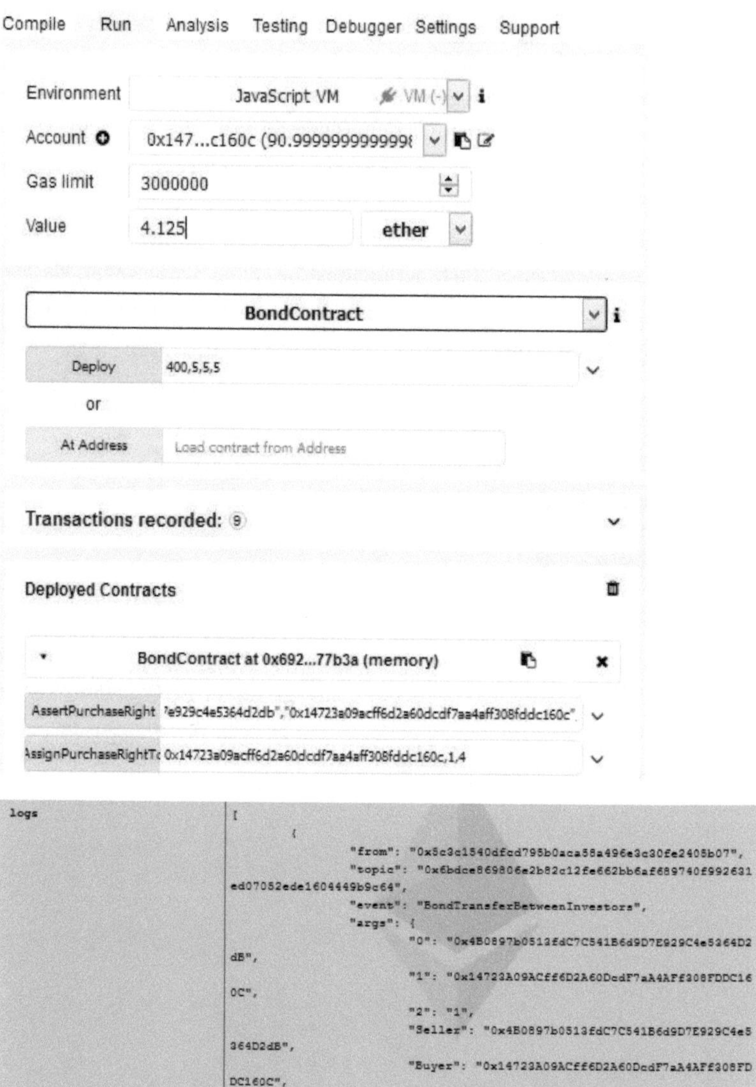

The next step involves the actual exchange of assets. The potential purchaser of the token can call the *AssertPurchaseRight* function by giving three arguments: The seller's address, the purchaser's address and the amount of token he intends to acquire in this exact order. He must attach the acquisition price of 4.125 Ether to the transaction message, including the compensation amount for *Investor B*'s forfeited coupon payment. In the same moment the purchase right lapses. Note, that the *AssertPurchaseRight* does not necessarily need to be called by the purchaser, but can also be called by other accounts on behalf of the purchaser too, provided that the purchase price is transferred. A successfully asserting of the token trade means, that also the fifth required function and event 1 for the ERC20 standard are implemented.

To check whether the trade has been successful, the balances of both investor's addresses should display the ownership of three Bond Token and the corresponding 15 Ether as *SumOfFaeValues*.

Assuming the maturity date has arrived, after transferring all coupon payments and face values, the account balances for each investor display the output described in the following sections.

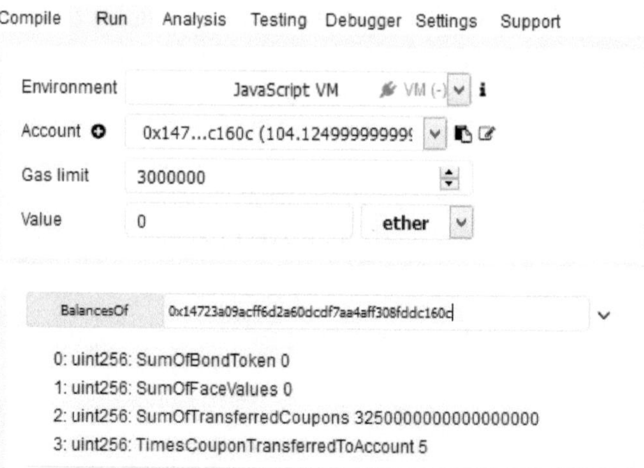

Investor A possesses zero Bond Token after maturity. The total value of transferred coupons from the issuer amount to 3.25 Ether, as calculated in table 6. After compensating *B* with 0.125 Ether for the forfeited coupon payment of the traded Bond Token, and gaining 1 Ether by paying only 4 Ether for a bond whose face value equals 5 Ether, *A*'s account balances is worth 104.1249 Ether.

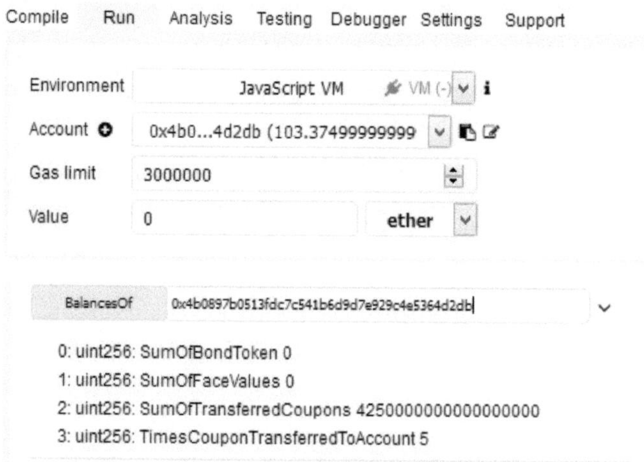

Investor B's Ether account balance reveals an amount of 103.37499 Ether, which equals the sum of the 100 Ether he owned from start, plus the transferred coupon payments by *issuer X* of 4.25 Ether and the compensation of 0.125 Ether he received from *investor A,* minus the 1 Ether he has lost by selling a bond with 5 Ether face value for 4 Ether.

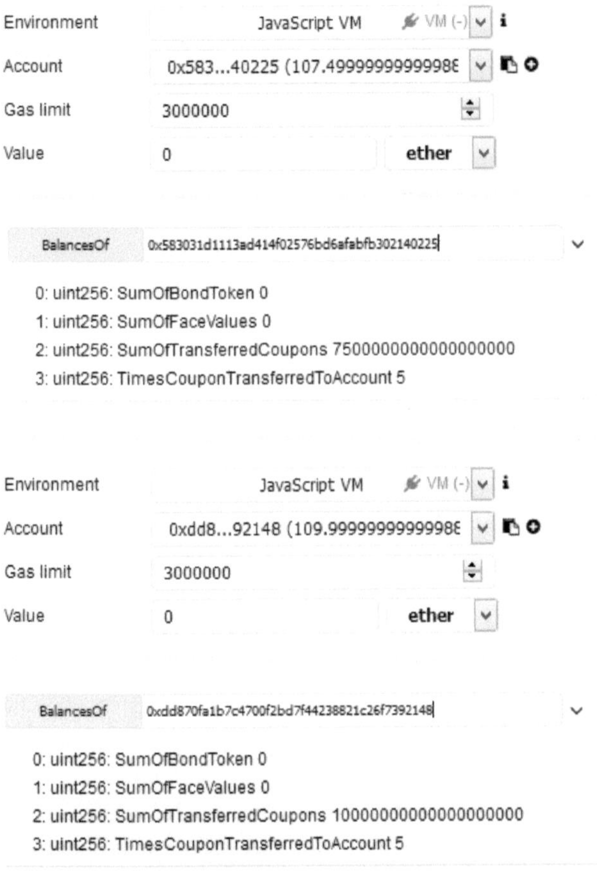

The balances for investors *C* and *D* are exactly the same as after all periods in simulation one, as indicated by table 6.

8 Evaluation of the smart contract

The conclusion that can be drawn from the simulations is that the program code of the developed *Bond Token* smart contract successfully enables to:

- input the bond's key data
- create tokens to which this bond key data can be assigned
- purchase these *Bond Tokens* from an *issuer* account
- trade *Bond Tokens* between *investor* accounts
- transfer coupon values
- repay face values
- meet the ERC20 token standard

Therefore the contract meet all requirements defined in chapter 4. Due to the author's lack of practical experience and the very limited test environment, this can only be seen as an indication of the applicability of smart contracts for the issuance and trading of bonds.

One of the major weaknesses of this contract is rooted in Solidity's incapability to support fixed-point values, what makes it impossible to specify a percentage in tenths or hundredths of a percent accuracy, without resorting to the user-unfriendly alternative of writing decimal numbers without decimal point. (https://solidity.readthedocs.io/ (2019m)) In the elaborated Bond Token contract the coupon rate must be inserted as integer. A workaround could be to change the code in the way that the decimal point can be omitted when entering the coupon rate in hundredths or tenths of a percent of accuracy. So that you enter 535 instead of 5.35 percent, and additionally change all affected equations within the script by dividing them by 100. In fact, that's how an intermediate version of the contract was designed, but it was altered for reasons of consistency and simplicity. The same incapability lead to an imprecise result for the yield. Because the decimal places for the values of the remaining time in years, the bond price in percent and also the displayed yield result itself are truncated. (https://ethereum.stackexchange.com (2018a))

Furthermore, yet, Solidity does not provide a way to fully automate the coupons payments or the repayment, because there is no way that a function executes itself regularly. Since in the current contract version, the coupon assignment and the repayment of the loan are manual steps, these processes are error-prone. It might be possible in the future using an oracle or an alarm clock service, to at least semiautomate these transfers. (https://ethereum.stackexchange.com (2018b)) The contract could make use of oracle services to request market data, like the market interest level or exchange rates in order to improve the usability. The maturity date could be converted into a more conventional format and the developed smart contract can only be used for this bond type also to improve the user-friendliness.

The smart contract was only deployed in a sandbox blockchain of Remix, and not tested in the *Ethereum Mainnet*. Since, not the most current version of Solidity has been used, malfunctions could occur, when the contract is deployed to the *Mainnet*.

Legal aspects were not taken into account in the development of the contract. Before such a smart contract could be used by companies and their investors, regulators would need to examine whether the smart contract meets regulatory requirements. (BaFin (2017)) The complex processes of a real world bond issuance and bond trading have been simplified within the simulations. The issuing company needs to choose the bond related data such as the face value, the coupon interest and the term on their own. This is a rather unrealistic assumption, as market expertise is required to determine these figures in order to offer an attractive security investment.

References

Altrogge, G. (1996). *Investition*. Oldenbourg Verlag GmbH. Munich. 4th edition.

Antonopoulos, A. (2017). *Mastering Bitcoin. Programming the Open Blockchain*. O'Reilly Media Inc. Sebastopol. 2nd edition.

Biryukov A., Khovratovich D., Tikhomirov S. (2017) Findel: Secure Derivative Contracts for Ethereum. In: Brenner M. et al. (eds) *Financial Cryptography and Data Security*. FC 2017. Lecture Notes in Computer Science. Springer, Cham, vol 10323.

Dannen, C. (2017). *Introducing Ethereum and Solidity. Foundations of Cryptocurrency and Blockchain Programming for Beginners*. Apress Media, LLC. New York. 1st edition.

Laurence, T. (2017). *Blockchain For Dummies*. John Wiley & Sons, Inc. Hoboken. 2nd edition.

Pavlus, J. (2018). Die Welt des Bitcoin. *Spektrum der Wissenschaft*. Spezial 3.18, pp. 56-64

Ross, S., Westerfield, R., Jordan, B. (2008). Corporate Finance Fundamentals. The McGraw-Hill Higher Education. New York. 8th edition.

Tapscott, D., Tapscott, A. (2017). *Die Blockchain-Revolution: Wie die Technologie hinter Bitcoin nicht nur das Finanzwesen verändert, sondern die ganze Welt*. Plassen Verlag. Kulmbach. 3rd edition.

Internet references

Atzler, E. (2017). *Daimler und die LBBW proben für die Zukunft.* https://www.handelsblatt.com/finanzen/banken-versicherungen/bitcoin-technik-blockchain-daimler-und-die-lbbw-proben-fuer-die-zukunft/19994182.html?ticket=ST-1095325-ZqfyP1X57x1WDQMfcZI5-ap4. (Retrieved June 04, 2018)

Azimdoust, N. (2019). *ERC20 Token Standard einfach erklärt.* https://blockchainwelt.de/erc20-token-ethereum-einfach-erklaert/ (Retrieved January 14, 2019)

BaFin (2017). *Blockchain Technologie.* https://www.bafin.de/DE/Aufsicht/FinTech/Blockchain/blockchain_node.html (Retrieved March 05, 2019)

Buterin, V. (2013). *Ethereum: A Next Generation Smart Contract & Decentralized Application Platform.* https://github.com/ethereum/wiki/wiki/Ethereum-White-Paper (Retrieved June 23, 2018)

Crypto, A. (2019). *Ethereum ditching Solidity for Vyper?* https://medium.com/swlh/ethereum-ditching-solidity-for-vyper-6db70fd7754 (Retrieved March 11, 2019)

Deutsche Bundesbank (2018). *Blockbaster. Final Report.* https://www.bundesbank.de/resource/blob/766672/29feab3f9079540441e3abda1ed2d2c1/mL/2018-10-25-blockbaster-final-report-data.pdf (Retrieved October 21, 2018)

Dourlens, J (2017). *SafeMath to protect from Overflow.* https://ethereum-dev.io/safemath-protect-overflows/ (Retrieved February 17, 2019)

European Banking Authority (2019). *Report with advice for the European Commission. On Crypto-Assets.* https://eba.europa.eu/documents/10180/2545547/EBA+Report+on+crypto+assets.pdf (Retrieved March 10, 2019)

European Central Bank (2018). *Cryptocurrencies and Tokens* https://www.ecb.europa.eu/paym/groups/pdf/fxcg/2018/20180906/Item_2a_-_Cryptocurrencies_and_tokens.pdf (Retrieved March 25, 2019)

https://solidity.readthedocs.io/ (2019a). Structure of a Contract. solidity.readthedocs.io/structure-of-a-contract.html#functions (Retrieved December 01, 2018)

https://solidity.readthedocs.io/ (2019b). Visibility and Getters. solidity.readthedocs.io/contracts.html#visibility-and-getters (Retrieved January 02, 2019)

https://solidity.readthedocs.io/ (2019c). *Function Modifiers.* solidity.readthedocs.io/contracts.html#function-modifiers (Retrieved January 12, 2019)

https://solidity.readthedocs.io/ (2019d). *Address Literals.* https://solidity.readthedocs.io/en/develop/types.html#address-literals (Retrieved February 18, 2019)

https://solidity.readthedocs.io/ (2019e). *Structs.* solidity.readthedocs.io/types.html#structs (Retrieved February 25, 2019)

https://solidity.readthedocs.io/ (2019f). *Mapping Types.* solidity.readthedocs.io/types.html#mapping-types (Retrieved February 26, 2019)

https://solidity.readthedocs.io/ (2019g). *Arrays.* solidity.readthedocs.io/types.html#arrays (Retrieved February 25, 2019)

https://solidity.readthedocs.io/ (2019h). *Introduction to Smart Contracts.* solidity.readthedocs.io/introduction-to-smart-contracts.html (Retrieved February 25, 2019)

https://solidity.readthedocs.io/ (2019i). *Variable Declaration.* solidity.readthedocs.io/style-guide.html#variable-declarations (Retrieved February 25, 2019)

https://solidity.readthedocs.io/ (2019j). *Creating Contracts.* solidity.readthedocs.io/contracts.html#creating-contracts (Retrieved February 25, 2019)

https://solidity.readthedocs.io/ (2019k). *Solidity by Example.* solidity.readthedocs.io/solidity-by-example.html (Retrieved February 25, 2019)

https://solidity.readthedocs.io/ (2019l). *Special Variables and Functions.* solidity.readthedocs.io/units-and-global-variables.html#block-and-transaction-properties (Retrieved January 23, 2019)

https://solidity.readthedocs.io/ (2019m). *Fix Point Numbers.* https://solidity.readthedocs.io/en/develop/types.html#fixed-point-numbers (Retrieved January 23, 2019)

https://remix.readthedocs.io/en/latest/ (2019a). *Welcome to Remix Documentation.* https://remix.readthedocs.io/en/latest/ (Retrieved March 02, 2019)

https://remix.readthedocs.io/en/latest/ (2019b). *Solidity Editor.* https://remix.readthedocs.io/en/latest/solidity_editor.html (Retrieved March 02, 2019)

https://remix.readthedocs.io/en/latest/ (2019c). *Compiling Contracts.* https://remix.readthedocs.io/en/latest/compile_tab.html (Retrieved March 02, 2019)

https://remix.readthedocs.io/en/latest/ (2019d). *File Explorer.* https://remix.readthedocs.io/en/latest/file_explorer.html (Retrieved March 02, 2019)

https://remix.readthedocs.io/en/latest/ (2019e). *Quick Start using the JavaScript VM.* https://remix.readthedocs.io/en/latest/quickstart_javascript_vm.html (Retrieved March 02, 2019)

https://remix.readthedocs.io/en/latest/ (2019f). *Run Setup.* https://remix.readthedocs.io/en/latest/run_tab.html#run-setup (Retrieved March 02, 2019)

https://remix.readthedocs.io/en/latest/ (2019g). *Terminal.* https://remix.readthedocs.io/en/latest/terminal.html (Retrieved January 23, 2019)

https://ethereum.stackexchange.com (2018a). *How can I represent decimal values in Solidity?* https://ethereum.stackexchange.com/questions/2987/how-can-i-represent-decimal-values-in-solidity (Retrieved January 23, 2019)

https://ethereum.stackexchange.com (2018b). *How can a contract run itself at a later time?* https://ethereum.stackexchange.com/questions/42/how-can-a-contract-run-itself-at-a-later-time (Retrieved January 23, 2019)

Nakamoto, S. (2008). *Bitcoin: A Peer-to-Peer Electronic Cash System.* https://bitcoin.org/bitcoin.pdf (Retrieved July 16, 2018)

Nasdaq (2015). *Nasdaq Linq Enables First-Ever Private Securities Issuance Documented With Blockchain Technology.* http://ir.nasdaq.com/static-files/db6368ec-8f14-451e-9c53-f78e0470191a (Retrieved July 30, 2018)

Proebsting, T. (2018a). *Writing a Simple Dividend Token Contract.* https://programtheblockchain.com/posts/2018/02/07/writing-a-simple-dividend-token-contract/ (Retrieved November 10, 2018)

Proebsting, T. (2018b). *Writing an ERC20 Token Contract.* https://programtheblockchain.com/posts/2018/01/30/writing-an-erc20-token-contract/ (Retrieved November 10, 2018)

Schütte, J. et al. (2017). *Blockchain und Smart Contracts. Technologie, For-schungsfragen und Anwendungen.* Fraunhofer-Gesellschaft. https://www.sit.fraunhofer.de/fileadmin/dokumente/studien_und_tech-nical_reports/Fraunhofer-Positionspapier_Blockchain-und-Smart-Contracts.pdf?_=1516641660 (Retrieved August 20, 2018)

Szabo, N. (1994). *Smart Contracts.* http://web.ar-chive.org/web/20160306112751/http://szabo.best.vwh.net/smart.con-tracts.html (Retrieved February 5, 2019)

The Economist (2015). *The promise of the blockchain: The trust machine.* https://www.economist.com/leaders/2015/10/31/the-trust-machine (Retrieved August 17, 2018)

w. a.: (2017). *Blockchain für die Wertpapier-Abwicklung.* https://www.wiwo.de/finanzen/boerse/australische-boerse-blockchain-fuer-die-wertpapier-abwicklung/20682908.html (Retrieved December 15, 2018)

w. a.: (2018). *ERC20 Token Standard.* https://theethereum.wiki/w/in-dex.php/ERC20_Token_Standard (Retrieved April 15, 2019)

w. a.: (2017). *Natural Unit.* https://theethereum.wiki/w/index.php/Natu-ral_Units (Retrieved January 23, 2019)

w. a.: (2017). *Remix.* https://theethereum.wiki/w/index.php/Remix (Retrieved January 23, 2019)

w. a.: (w. y.). Solidity Events. https://www.bitdegree.org/learn/solidity-events (Retrieved January 23, 2019)

Will it Scale-Channel (2017a). Learning Solidity: Tutorial 6 Data Types (Array, Mapping, Struct). https://www.youtube.com/watch?v=8UhO3IKApSg&t=841s (Retrieved February 15, 2019)

Will it Scale-Channel (2017b). *Learning Solidity: Tutorial 3 Custom Modifiers and Error Handling.* https://www.youtube.com/watch?v=3Ob-TNzDM3wI&list=PL16WqdAj66SCOdL6XIFbke-XQg2GW_Avg&index=3 (Retrieved February 16, 2019)

Will it Scale-Channel (2017c). *Learning Solidity: Tutorial 28 Address book on the blockchain powered by Angular.* https://www.youtube.com/watch?v=bvxKICus3bw&list=PL16WqdAj66SCOdL6XIFbke-XQg2GW_Avg&index=28 (Retrieved February 16, 2019)

Will it Scale-Channel (2017d). *Learning Solidity: Tutorial 9 ERC20 Tokens and Creating your own Cryptocurrency.* https://www.youtube.com/watch?v=r7XojpI-DuhA&list=PL16WqdAj66SCOdL6XIFbke-XQg2GW_Avg&index=9 (Retrieved February 16, 2019)

Appendix

```solidity
1   pragma solidity ^0.4.24;
2
3   // this smart contract enables companies to generate funds from investors
4   // without intermediary by issuing a blockchain equivalent to a fixed-interest coupon bond
5   // it also allows the investors to trade the bond token
6
7   contract BondContract {
8
9       string public name = "Company X ERC20 Bond Token Emission No.1";
10      string public symbol = "XEBTENo.1";
11
12      struct AccountBondData{  // builds a structure with four variables reflecting bond related data of each investor account
13
14          uint256 SumOfBondToken;
15          uint256 SumOfFaceValues;
16          uint256 SumOfTransferredCoupons;
17          uint256 TimesCouponTransferredToAccount;
18          }
19
20      struct PurchaseOfferData{ // builds a structure representing the offer data of a potential trade
21          uint256 AmountOfOfferedBondToken;
22          uint256 TradingPricePerBondTokenInWei;
23          uint256 Yield;
24      }
25
26      // declaration of variables
27      address public Issuer;
28      address Investor;
29      address[] Investors;
30
31      mapping(address=>AccountBondData) public BalancesOf;
32      mapping(address => mapping(address => uint256)) PurchaseRight;
33      mapping(address => mapping(address => PurchaseOfferData)) public MyOfferData;
34
35      uint8   decimals = 18;
36      uint256 public TotalBondTokenSupply;
37      uint256 IssuanceVolumeInWei;
38      uint256 public LeftToReachIssuanceVolumeGoalInWei;
39      uint256 public BondTokenCouponInPercent;
40      uint256 public BondTokenFaceValueInEther;
41      uint256 BondTokenTradingPriceInEther;
42      uint256 BondTokenTradingPriceInWei;
43      uint256 BondTokenTradingPriceInPercent;
44      uint256 BondTokenFaceValueInWei;
45      uint256 n;
46      uint256 TransactionPrice;
47      uint256 TransferAmount;
48      uint256 public TermInYears;
49      uint256 TermInSeconds;
50      uint256 TermInDays;
51      uint256 TimeOfContractCreation = now;
52      uint256 EndOfTokensSale;
53      uint256 public MaturityDateInSecondsSinceUnixEpoch;
54      uint256 RemainingTermInYears;
55
56      event BondPurchaseFromIssuer(address Investor, uint256 TokenAmount, uint256 BondsTotalFaceValue);
57      event AssignedRight(address indexed Owner, address indexed Beneficiary, uint256 TokenAmount);
58      event BondTransferBetweenInvestors(address indexed Seller, address indexed Buyer, uint256 TokenAmount);
59
60      constructor(uint256 _IssuanceVolumeInEther, uint256 _BondTokenFaceValueInEther,uint256 _CouponInPercent, uint256 _TermInYears) payable {
61          LeftToReachIssuanceVolumeGoalInWei = safeMultiplication(_IssuanceVolumeInEther,(uint256(10) ** decimals));
62          IssuanceVolumeInWei = safeMultiplication(_IssuanceVolumeInEther,(uint256(10) ** decimals));
63          BondTokenFaceValueInWei = safeMultiplication(_BondTokenFaceValueInEther,(uint256(10) ** decimals));
64          BondTokenFaceValueInEther = _BondTokenFaceValueInEther;
65          BondTokenCouponInPercent = _CouponInPercent;
66
67          TermInYears = _TermInYears;
68          TermInSeconds = safeMultiplication(TermInYears, 365 days);
69          MaturityDateInSecondsSinceUnixEpoch = safeAddition(now, TermInSeconds);
70
71          EndOfTokensSale = safeAddition(TimeOfContractCreation,1 days);
72
73          TotalBondTokenSupply = safeDivision(IssuanceVolumeInWei, BondTokenFaceValueInWei);
74          Issuer = msg.sender;
75          BalancesOf[Issuer].SumOfBondToken = TotalBondTokenSupply;
```

```solidity
76
77          }
78
79          // enables investors to buy Bond Token from issuer
80 -        function BuyBondTokenFromIssuer(uint256 _TokenAmount) public payable returns(bool success) {
81              var investor = BalancesOf[msg.sender];
82              TransactionPrice = safeMultiplication(BondTokenFaceValueInWei, _TokenAmount);
83
84              require(LeftToReachIssuanceVolumeGoalInWei>=TransactionPrice);
85              require(TransactionPrice == msg.value);
86              require(now <= EndOfTokensSale);
87
88              LeftToReachIssuanceVolumeGoalInWei -= TransactionPrice;
89              investor.SumOfFaceValues += TransactionPrice;
90              investor.SumOfBondToken += _TokenAmount;
91              BalancesOf[Issuer].SumOfBondToken -= _TokenAmount;
92
93              n = Investors.length;
94 -            for(uint i = 0; i < n; i++) {
95              if (Investors[i] == msg.sender) return false;
96              }
97
98              Investors.push(msg.sender);
99
100             emit BondPurchaseFromIssuer(msg.sender, _TokenAmount, TransactionPrice);
101
102             return true;
103         }
104
105         // enables issuer to transfer interests to a specific investor account
106 -       function TransferCouponsToOneInvestor(address _InvestorAccountAddress) public OnlyIssuer returns(bool success){
107             var investor = BalancesOf[_InvestorAccountAddress];
108             Investor = _InvestorAccountAddress;
109             require(investor.TimesCouponTransferredToAccount < TermInYears);
110             TransferAmount = safeDivision((safeMultiplication(BalancesOf[Investor].SumOfFaceValues,(BondTokenCouponInPercent))),100);
111             Investor.transfer(TransferAmount);
112             investor.SumOfTransferredCoupons += TransferAmount;
113             investor.TimesCouponTransferredToAccount += 1;

114
115             return true;
116         }
117
118         // enables issuer to transfer interests to all investor accounts at once
119 -       function TransferCouponsToAllInvestors () public OnlyIssuer returns(bool success){
120             n = Investors.length;
121 -           for(uint256 i=0;i<n;i++){
122             Investor = Investors[i];
123             require(BalancesOf[Investor].TimesCouponTransferredToAccount < TermInYears);
124             TransferAmount = safeDivision((safeMultiplication(BalancesOf[Investor].SumOfFaceValues,(BondTokenCouponInPercent))),100).
125             Investor.transfer(TransferAmount);
126             BalancesOf[Investor].SumOfTransferredCoupons += TransferAmount;
127             BalancesOf[Investor].TimesCouponTransferredToAccount += 1;
128             }
129
130             return true;
131         }
132
133         // enables issuer to transfer bonds face value to a specific investor account at maturity
134 -       function TransferFaceValueToOneInvestor (address _InvestorAccountAddress) public OnlyIssuer returns(bool success){
135             require(now>= MaturityDateInSecondsSinceUnixEpoch);
136             var investor = BalancesOf[_InvestorAccountAddress];
137             Investor = _InvestorAccountAddress;
138             TransferAmount = investor.SumOfFaceValues;
139             Investor.transfer(TransferAmount);
140             investor.SumOfFaceValues -= TransferAmount;
141             BalancesOf[Issuer].SumOfBondToken += investor.SumOfBondToken;
142             investor.SumOfBondToken = 0;
143
144             return true;
145         }
146
147         // enables issuer to transfer face values of the bond to all investor accounts at once
148 -       function TransferFaceValuesToAllInvestors () public OnlyIssuer returns(bool success){
149             require(now>= MaturityDateInSecondsSinceUnixEpoch);
150             n = Investors.length;
151 -           for(uint256 i=0;i<n;i++){
```

```
152             Investor = Investors[i];
153             TransferAmount = BalancesOf[Investor].SumOfFaceValues;
154             Investor.transfer(TransferAmount);
155             BalancesOf[Investor].SumOfFaceValues -= TransferAmount;
156             BalancesOf[Issuer].SumOfBondToken -= BalancesOf[Investor].SumOfBondToken;
157             BalancesOf[Investor].SumOfBondToken = 0;
158             }
159
160         return true;
161     }
162
163     // Necessity for ERC20 Token-Standard
164     // enables an Investor (Token owner) to assign a purchase right to buy his Bond Token to another address
165 -   function AssignPurchaseRightTo(address Purchaser, uint256 TokenAmount, uint256 TradingPricePerBondTokenInEther) public returns (bool success) {
166         require(TokenAmount <= BalancesOf[msg.sender].SumOfBondToken);
167         PurchaseRight[msg.sender][Purchaser] = TokenAmount;
168         MyOfferData[msg.sender][Purchaser].AmountOfOfferedBondToken = TokenAmount;
169
170         BondTokenTradingPriceInWei = safeMultiplication(TradingPricePerBondTokenInEther,(uint256(10) ** decimals));
171         BondTokenTradingPriceInPercent = safeDivision(safeMultiplication(BondTokenTradingPriceInWei, 100), BondTokenFaceValueInWei);
172
173         RemainingTermInYears = (MaturityDateInSecondsSinceUnixEpoch - now) / 365 days;
174
175 -       if (BondTokenTradingPriceInWei == 0){
176             MyOfferData[msg.sender][Purchaser].TradingPricePerBondTokenInWei = BondTokenFaceValueInWei;
177         }
178 -       else {
179         MyOfferData[msg.sender][Purchaser].TradingPricePerBondTokenInWei = BondTokenTradingPriceInWei;
180         }
181
182         MyOfferData[msg.sender][Purchaser].Yield = (((BondTokenCouponInPercent) +
183         ((100 - BondTokenTradingPriceInPercent) / RemainingTermInYears)) * 100) /  BondTokenTradingPriceInPercent;
184
185
186         emit AssignedRight(msg.sender, Purchaser, TokenAmount);
187         return true;
188     }
189
190     // Necessity for ERC20 Token-Standard
191     // enables the owner of a purchase right to make use of it and buy Bond Token from another investor
192 -   function AssertPurchaseRight(address Seller, address Purchaser, uint256 TokenAmount) public payable returns (bool success) {
193         require(Seller != Purchaser);
194         require(Purchaser != address(0));
195
196         require(TokenAmount <= PurchaseRight[Seller][Purchaser]);
197 -       if (BondTokenTradingPriceInWei == 0){
198             require(msg.value >= safeMultiplication(TokenAmount, BondTokenFaceValueInWei));
199         }
200         else require(msg.value >= safeMultiplication(TokenAmount, BondTokenTradingPriceInWei));
201
202
203         BalancesOf[Seller].SumOfBondToken -= TokenAmount;
204         BalancesOf[Seller].SumOfFaceValues -= safeMultiplication(TokenAmount, BondTokenFaceValueInWei); // msg.value
205
206         BalancesOf[Purchaser].SumOfBondToken += TokenAmount;
207         BalancesOf[Purchaser].SumOfFaceValues += safeMultiplication(TokenAmount, BondTokenFaceValueInWei); // msg.value
208
209         PurchaseRight[Seller][Purchaser] -= TokenAmount;
210
211         Seller.transfer(msg.value);
212
213         MyOfferData[Seller][Purchaser].AmountOfOfferedBondToken -= TokenAmount;
214
215         emit BondTransferBetweenInvestors(Seller, Purchaser, TokenAmount);
216         return true;
217     }
218
219     // Necessity for ERC20 Token-Standard
220     // enables to send Bond Token to another address
221 -   function transferBondToken(address to, uint256 TokenAmount) public returns(bool success) {
222         require(BalancesOf[msg.sender].SumOfBondToken >= TokenAmount);
223         BalancesOf[msg.sender].SumOfBondToken -= TokenAmount;
224         BalancesOf[to].SumOfBondToken += TokenAmount;
```

```solidity
225
226        BalancesOf[msg.sender].SumOfFaceValues -= TokenAmount*BondTokenFaceValueInWei; // safeMultiplication
227        BalancesOf[to].SumOfFaceValues += TokenAmount*BondTokenFaceValueInWei;
228
229        emit BondTransferBetweenInvestors(msg.sender, to, TokenAmount);
230        return true;
231    }
232
233    // gives the contract's Ether balance
234    function ContractEtherBalance() public view returns (uint256) {
235        return address(this).balance;
236    }
237
238    // enables the issuer withdraw Ether from the contract
239    function WithdrawalOfContractOwner(uint256 WithdrawAmountInWei) public OnlyIssuer returns(bool success){
240        msg.sender.transfer(WithdrawAmountInWei);
241
242        return true;
243    }
244
245    // gives total amount of investors
246    function CountInvestors() view public returns (uint) {
247        return Investors.length;
248    }
249
250    // gives list of investors
251    function ListOfInvestors() view public returns (address[]) {
252        return Investors;
253    }
254
255    // enables issuer to transfer Ether to contract
256    function TransferEtherToContract () public payable OnlyIssuer {
257    }
258
259    // prevention from integer overflow
260    function safeMultiplication(uint256 a, uint256 b) internal pure returns (uint256) {
261        if (a == 0) {
262            return 0;
263        } else {
264            uint256 c = a * b;
265            assert(c / a == b);
266            return c;
267        }
268    }
269
270    // prevention from integer overflow
271    function safeDivision(uint256 a, uint256 b) internal pure returns (uint256) {
272        // Solidity only automatically asserts when dividing by 0
273        require(b > 0);
274        uint256 c = a / b;
275        assert(a == b * c + a % b); // There is no case in which this doesn't hold
276        return c;
277    }
278
279    // prevention from integer overflow
280    function safeAddition(uint256 a, uint256 b) internal pure returns (uint256) {
281        uint256 c = a + b;
282        require(c >= a);
283
284        return c;
285    }
286
287    // integration in other functions ensures that only the issuer can call this function
288    modifier OnlyIssuer() {
289        require(msg.sender == Issuer);
290        _;
291    }
292 }
293
```